THE S
CONSUMER'S
GUIDE
TO GOOD
CREDIT

How to Earn Good Credit in a Bad Economy

JOHN ULZHEIMER

WITH DEANNA TEMPLETON

ALLWORTH PRESS
NEW YORK

Allworth Press books may be purchased in bulk at special discounts
for sales promotion, corporate gifts, fund-raising, or educational purposes.
Special editions can also be created to specifications. For details,
contact the Special Sales Department, Allworth Press,
307 West 36th Street, 11th Floor, New York,
NY 10018 or info@skyhorsepublishing.com.

15 14 13 12 11   5 4 3 2 1

Published by Allworth Press
An imprint of Skyhorse Publishing
307 West 36th Street, 11th Floor,
New York, NY 10018.

Allworth Press® is a registered trademark of Skyhorse Publishing, Inc.®,
a Delaware corporation.
www.allworth.com

ISBN: 978-1-58115-904-2

Library of Congress Cataloging-in-Publication Data is available on file.

Printed in Canada

TABLE OF CONTENTS

Introduction:
A Note from John

Hello and welcome to my second book! I know you have countless choices when it comes to personal finance literature, and I'm honored and thrilled that you've chosen *The Smart Consumer's Guide to Good Credit* to be a part of your personal library. First, let me fill you in on my credit background.

ABOUT THE AUTHOR

I was born in Fort Rucker, Alabama, in 1968, the son of an Army officer. As with most Army brats, I moved around every few years until my family moved to Atlanta in the late '70s. My father retired, and Atlanta became "home." I went to Norcross High School and graduated in 1986. I collectively spent the next five years at Georgia Southern (now Georgia Southern University), the University of Tennessee, and West Georgia College (now the University of West Georgia.)

I graduated in 1991 with a degree in Criminal Justice. In '91 the job market in Atlanta was very poor. And because my graduation predated the Internet by a good decade, I was sending out hundreds of resumes to local companies via US mail. One of the companies that responded was Equifax. I had never heard of them and I had no clue what they did. They were just on "the list" of companies based in Atlanta.

I was granted an interview for a customer service position. I interviewed for the job and took a required typing test. The minimum acceptable word count for the typing test was thirty words per minute. I typed twenty-nine. My contact let me take the typing test again and again, and each time: twenty-nine words. Thankfully Equifax saw fit to let me slide, and I was hired in November 1991 as a customer service representative.

I spent the next six years learning everything there was to know about consumer credit reports: where the data came from, how it was reported, how it was normalized, how it was stored, what our legal obligations for maintaining data accuracy were, how the data was packaged and sold, and how lenders used the information to make decisions. I became "Fair Credit Reporting Act Certified" by the credit industry's trade association, which at that time was called the Associated Credit Bureaus. I resigned from the company in November 1997 to take a position with credit scoring giant Fair Isaac (FICO).

FICO was looking for someone in their Atlanta office to help manage the company's credit bureau–based scoring models. And since I had a deep credit reporting background and a decent knowledge of credit scoring tools, we had a mutual fit. I interviewed, didn't make a fool of myself, got the offer, and started at FICO in November 1997.

I spent the next seven years developing an expertise in credit scoring: how scores are calculated, how scoring systems are designed and developed, how scoring tools are implemented and validated. I also spent a lot of time speaking with consumers and consumer groups on how to improve their credit management practices so they could improve their credit scores. I resigned from FICO at the end of 2004, yet remain very close to many at the company still today.

In 2004 I started writing credit-related newsletters and manuals for an organization that helped people recover their credit after a bankruptcy. And in 2005 I started doing contract work for Credit.com, which included content and media-related work. I always tell people that in 2005 not many media folks cared about what I had to say about credit. This has certainly changed, and since 2007 I've been quoted and published well over 1,000 times by every mainstream media outlet you can name.

In late 2005 my career path took a strange turn, and I was asked to serve as an expert witness defending a small credit bureau in Baton Rouge, Louisiana. I enjoyed the work immensely and started to market myself as a credit expert witness, which has become a large part of my unique career path. At the end of 2011 I had been an expert witness in over 100 credit-related lawsuits and have been qualified by both federal and state courts as a credit expert. And finally, in 2011 I became "Fair Credit Reporting Act Certified" for a second time by the credit industry's trade association, which is now called the Consumer Data Industry Association.

When I left FICO in 2004, my goal was to give a little back to the consumer. Why? I chose that path because it was blatantly obvious that there was a need for credible and accurate credit education, or "*creducation*" as an old friend of mine calls it. And while one man certainly can't fill all of our creducation needs, one man can certainly try. And that's why I wrote this book, so enjoy.

Before you get started on the substantive portions, we need to set some ground rules. Read on . . .

GROUND RULES

1. My writing style has been called "*smart and smart-ass.*" I have no formal (or even informal) training as an author, which is actually a good thing, because credit is such a highly technical subject and needs a little spice.

2. I am not representing the credit industry. I am also *not* a consumer advocate, despite what some people have

called me. I defend industry practices, a lot. And I call them out, critically, where I think they've screwed up. I like to think of myself as an umpire simply calling balls and strikes—I don't care who wins.

3. I'm going to assume you have a basic understanding of consumer credit. This means I'm not going to bore you with the same retreaded drivel you read in almost every other credit-related book. I'm not going to explain what a credit report is. I'm not going to explain what a credit score is. That's Credit 101. This book is credit for PhD students.

4. What you're about to read is going to come across as harsh at times, but you need to read about these important topics in an unvarnished manner. Sugar coating credit-related advice is a waste of your time.

5. You shouldn't get emotional when reading this book. Why not? You shouldn't get emotional because the world of consumer credit is not based on relationships, friends, or history. It's based on a scientific and empirical evaluation of your risk as a potential borrower, and that tends to be very impersonal. I'll give you an example:

   Banks are not your friends, so don't expect them to act like they are. Last year Bank of America announced that they would implement a $59 annual fee on about 5 percent of their cardholder accounts. The reaction in the blog world was swift and emotional: *Outrageous! Illegal! Immoral!* One reader even called them "mean-spirited," yet a $59 annual fee is sixteen cents a day. It's less than you spend getting your hair done, going out to dinner, running up a bar tab, etc. In the grand scheme of things, $59 is a drop in your bucket.

   It's clear that many of us have unrealistic expectations when it comes to banks and credit card issuers.

These companies are *for profit* organizations. That means they're in it strictly for the money—your money. They don't care about your personal situations, they don't care about your excuses, they don't care that the dog ate your checkbook.

They want to be paid, they want to make money, they want to make *more* money, and they want it to come from *you*. The sooner we stop thinking about banks and credit card issuers like we think of our family and friends, the better off we'll be.

6. You have some responsibilities when it comes to financial services. In fact, it's your job to choose good bank products. Let me repeat that: *it's your job to ensure that the credit products you choose are actually good products*. DYODD = Do Your Own Due Diligence. I have a friend who sends me stock tips from time to time, and he always ends his emails with DYODD. What that means is: "Don't complain if you buy a dog." That same acronym applies to bank products.

    If monthly fees are going to be offensive to you, then don't choose pre-paid debit cards. If annual fees are going to bother you, then you probably shouldn't open a credit card, because there's no guarantee that your "no fee" card won't have an annual fee next year. If a $5 ATM fee is going to infuriate you, then don't use that bank's ATM machines. And finally, if paying interest is going to drive you crazy, then don't revolve balances. Avoiding offensive bank products is actually quite easy if you DYODD.

7. For most of you, getting into debt was your choice. I know, I know, you didn't ask to lose your job and you have to survive and credit cards are your only way to pay. That's a reasonable, if not fully acceptable, excuse for being in debt. But "The banks kept giving me more credit cards" is not. In general, pulling out

that little piece of plastic and swiping it is a voluntary act, regardless of how or why it got in your wallet. If you don't want to get into debt, then don't use credit. Trust me, I'm fully aware that some people are addicted to credit cards. For those people, avoidance is the right strategy—and you know that was hard for me to write.

8. And finally, credit is a privilege, not a right. This has to be my favorite one. How many advertisements for credit (and insurance) have you seen or heard with the tagline "Get the savings you deserve"? I can assure you that no bank or insurance company believes that you *deserve* anything. Further, if you want to do business with them, you'll have to earn the privilege of doing so.

You don't "deserve" a card, a mortgage loan, a car loan, or any other credit-related product. Remember, at the end of every dollar you borrow from a bank—there's an investor. That investor might be the federal government, a hedge fund, a pension fund, a nonprofit organization, or a consumer.

Now that we've set those ground rules . . . *enjoy*!

PART I

Credit Reports

CHAPTER 1

Credit Reporting Agencies: What You Didn't Know

Equifax, TransUnion, and Experian—we all know these guys. I've written about them hundreds of times over the past decade. We "credit guys" tend to focus on these companies for obvious reasons, but what you may not know is that they're not the only companies that are keeping an eye on you.

Let's set this up: the Fair Credit Reporting Act actually doesn't refer to Equifax, TransUnion, and Experian as *credit reporting agencies*. They're actually referred to as *consumer reporting agencies*, meaning they create reports for sale to third parties, which will be used as a basis for some sort of decision-making process. This is usually credit or employment, but can also include things like insurance or housing.

The Big Three credit reporting agencies are not the only companies who do this. In fact, there are at least three more companies that have similar business models and maintain, own, or otherwise profit from storing and selling your information to others. These companies are Computer Sciences Corporation,

Innovis Data Solutions, and ChoicePoint. Let's dissect who they are, what they do, and how you can get a copy of what they have in their systems on you.

1. COMPUTER SCIENCES CORPORATION

These guys are better known as CSC and are traded on the NYSE under the symbol CSC. They are based in Virginia and do business in over ninety countries and across multiple industries, including consumer credit reporting. Their credit arm is known as CSC Credit Services, and they are what is referred to as an independent consumer reporting agency, or system affiliate.

They own a significant percentage of the credit files on the Equifax database, mostly belonging to consumers living in the Midwest and Central states including Texas, Oklahoma, Nebraska, Arkansas, Indiana, Kansas, Missouri, Iowa, Wisconsin, and Minnesota. So for those of you living from Texas straight up to the Dakotas, your credit file from Equifax is actually a CSC credit report. That means your CSC file is maintained and sold by Equifax, but CSC updates any disputes and disclosures, and shares in any revenue generated by the sale of your credit report.

If you suspect you live in a CSC state or zip code, you can request a copy of your credit report for free, once a year, here:

CSC Credit Services
Consumer Assistance
P.O. Box 619054
Dallas, TX 75261-9054
(800) 759-5979
www.csccredit.com

2. INNOVIS DATA SOLUTIONS

These guys are commonly known as the "fourth" credit bureau. They used to be called CBC, which stands for the Credit

Bureau of Columbus (Ohio). CBC used to be a very large Equifax system affiliate, much like CSC is currently. However, CBC eventually chose to stand on their own and further built out their own credit reporting database by acquisition.

Today, they are a national credit bureau, but their data is not as complete as the data provided by the Big Three. Point being, you have an Innovis credit report, regardless of where you live, but it's not nearly as comprehensive as your other credit reports. Also, there is no FICO score for the Innovis credit report, and because most lenders base their decisions, in part, on a FICO score, the lack thereof makes it difficult or impossible for lenders to use their credit reports.

If you'd like to claim your free copy of your Innovis credit report, you can do so by phone or mail:

Phone: Call 1-800-540-2505 any time to request a copy of your Innovis Credit Report using their automated system. Representatives are available to assist you Monday through Friday, 8 a.m.–8 p.m. EST.

Mail: Complete the online Credit Report Request Form at www.innovis.com/InnovisWeb/formOrderReport.html and mail it to:

Innovis
Attn: Consumer Assistance
P.O. Box 1689
Pittsburgh, PA 15230-1689

3. CHOICEPOINT

These guys have an interesting history, especially for a credit junkie like me. Follow me on this SAT/ACT-style analogy: Equifax is to lenders as ChoicePoint is to insurance companies and employers. ChoicePoint, who many years ago was the insurance services division of Equifax, and is now owned by LexisNexis, isn't a credit reporting agency, but they are a consumer reporting agency.

They sell reports and scores to insurance companies and reports to employers who use that data to determine whether or not they want to hire or insure you. ChoicePoint is also the poster child for corporate data breaches. In 2004 their database was breached, not by hackers but by a group of fraudsters who set up what appeared to be legitimate insurance company accounts, which allowed to them to access ChoicePoint's databases just as easily as any other legitimate insurance company.

The reports that ChoicePoint sells to insurance companies are called CLUE reports (Comprehensive Loss Underwriting Exchange). These are essentially a listing of any homeowner or auto insurance claims you've made in the past seven years. The scores they sell to insurance companies used to be called CP-Attract scores, and are now called LexisNexis Attract scores, given the new ownership of the company. They are designed to predict insurance risk.

In addition to the CLUE reports, they also sell reports to employers detailing your employment history. And finally, they sell reports to landlords about your previous tenancy history. There are no scores included with the employment or tenant reports. And, if no company has requested or reported anything to them, then your reports will be empty or clear. For example, I haven't filed a homeowner or auto claim in the past seven years, so my CLUE reports are empty.

You can access your CLUE reports, your employment history report, and your resident history report once every twelve months at no cost by visiting the LexisNexis site for personal reports at https://personalreports.lexisnexis.com/.

WHAT CREDIT REPORTING AGENCIES WON'T LET YOU DO, AND WHY NOT

We all know what the credit reporting agencies will allow consumers to do. They'll let you either purchase your credit reports or claim freebies periodically because of state and federal laws. They'll let you place fraud alerts on your credit files if you feel like you may have been exposed to identity theft. And they'll even let you place a short statement on your credit report if you want to explain your side of the story vis-à-vis an item with which you don't agree.

However, there are several things they will not allow you to do under almost any circumstance:

Add Accounts to Your Own Credit Reports

The credit reporting agencies are all for-profit businesses, which means they're in it to make money. The companies that they allow to report information into their databases pay them, in some way, for the privilege of doing so. These companies, legally referred to as "data furnishers," must either buy credit reports from the credit bureaus or pay a fee to the credit bureaus as a "data furnisher only." I know of several collection agencies that do not buy traditional credit reports from the bureaus, but do pay a fee to furnish data to them.

And because you are neither a data furnisher nor a buyer of credit reports, the credit bureaus are not going to allow you to add accounts to your credit files. You might ask, "Why would I want to do such a thing anyway?" The answer is quite simple: because your traditional credit files do not contain a record of all of your payment obligations. Think of things like apartment or home rental payments, utility payments, gym membership payments, or any other recurring obligations you pay on time each and every month. You're not getting credit for that credit. I've even had people argue that they view tithing as an obligation, yet they get no "credit report" credit for it. Who am I to argue with them?

Report Accounts of People Who Owe You Money

This one is very similar to the first one above. You are not allowed, as a non–data furnisher, to report the payment activity of other people who either owe you money or otherwise make payments to you each month. Think about people who are your roommates or tenants in rental properties. It would be great to report them to the credit bureaus each month as either making their payments on time or not.

The reason you're not allowed to do so is because you're simply too small, a one-man shop, so to speak. The credit bureaus don't want to fuss with a landlord who wants to report one or two rental obligations to them each month. They're set up as a volume shop, meaning they want a large volume of reporting each month. And frankly, they're doing you a favor by not accepting your "accounts." Why? Because the minute you report something on a credit file, you become liable to the Fair Credit Reporting Act and its eighty-four pages of rules, regulations, and obligations. Trust me, you're not interested in dealing with that mess.

Your alternative: do a really good job screening tenants and roommates up front so you don't have to leverage credit reporting to ensure on-time payments.

Pull Credit Reports on Other People

The credit reporting agencies will not grant you access to their databases to pull credit reports on people other than yourself unless you have a darn good legal reason for doing so, and even then they may simply choose not to do business with you. Nobody has the right to pull credit reports—it's a privilege that the agencies guard closely. Again, if you own a home and want to rent out a room or have a rental property, you'd like to check credit reports prior to turning over the keys. But the credit bureaus don't see value in you buying one or two credit reports a year. And I can't disagree with them.

There are even articles about how couples should be allowed to pull each other's credit reports and scores before getting too seriously involved. And, again, I can't disagree. Regardless, those credit reports won't come directly from the bureaus. You're going to have to have that difficult conversation on your own, sans credit reports.

Your alternative: there are tenant-screening companies who will resell a credit report to you on a potential tenant. The cost is not terribly excessive, $20–$50 each, and that cost is generally absorbed or subsidized by the potential tenant as part of their application fee. You can also certainly request that the tenant buy their own credit reports and hand them over.

Remove Your Credit File from Their System or Otherwise Stop Maintaining a File on You

This topic is a lightening rod. Many, if not most, people do not like how the credit bureaus are able to collect, maintain, score, and sell your data without your permission. The reason for this discontent is simple: it's your data, regardless of how you want to slice the argument. You have the mortgage with Chase. You have the credit card with Wells Fargo. You have the auto loan with Citibank. The lenders didn't force those loans on you. You chose to do business, and chose to do business with them. The accounts are yours.

There is also a long history of credit file inaccuracies and, frankly, credit bureau negligence. If only you could see what I can see, you'd realize that the credit bureaus find themselves on the wrong side of the FCRA and credit damage lawsuits hundreds of times each year. The trust just isn't there.

You simply don't have the authority to command the bureaus to stop collecting your data and selling it. There is nothing in any federal or state statute that gives you the right to do so. In fact, a lot of the data that bureaus maintain in files outside of their credit report databases is unregulated. That means anyone can buy it for any reason, and they can sell it to me regardless of how you feel about it.

The closest thing you've got to getting out of their system is the credit freeze, which restricts who can access your credit files and prevents new accounts from being opened in your name. This is an identity-theft prevention service, and it isn't a free service unless you've been a victim of fraud already. The "pay for freeze" services also aren't as advanced as credit monitoring services, and can be expensive and clunky to manage.

CHAPTER 2

Credit Reports: What's in Yours?

Credit reports are generally broken down into between five and seven areas, depending on which credit report you're looking at and whether it's a "consumer" version or a "lender" version. Here are the sections and what you're likely to find in each:

PERSONAL IDENTIFICATION DATA

This is where you're going to find your name, any variations of your name, current and former addresses, date of birth, social security number, and perhaps your current or previous employer.

INQUIRIES

This is a list of who has pulled your credit reports and on what date. The "consumer" version of the credit report is going to have all of your inquiries. The "lender" version is only going to have hard inquiries. We'll cover the difference between these types of inquiries in Chapter 10.

COLLECTIONS

There is a separate section on a credit report for third-party collections. This is not the internal collection department at your bank or credit card issuer. This is when your creditors have either sold or consigned your delinquent debts to an outside company for collection efforts.

TRADE

The trade section is going to make up the bulk of your credit report. This is where all of your accounts with lenders are going to show up. Sometimes they're called "trade lines" as well.

PUBLIC RECORDS

On some old credit report formats the public records section also houses third-party collections, despite the fact that a collection is hardly a public record. In the newer consumer versions they are called out as their own unique item, leaving the public record section to only house liens, judgments, and bankruptcies.

CONSUMER STATEMENT

You might not know this, but you have the right to add a short statement to your credit reports. In most states this is limited to no more than 100 words, so you'll need to bust out your best Twitter or text-messaging skills to fit an explanation of why you stopped paying on your credit cards.

So now that we know what you will see on your credit reports, let's address what you probably won't see on your credit reports. Under most circumstances you won't see:

GYM MEMBERSHIPS

These were reported at one time, but only when they went delinquent. Do you remember when gyms would sign people up for three- to five-year contracts and if you decided you were buff enough and cancelled, they'd try and hit you up for the full amount?

PUBLIC UTILITIES

You won't normally see your gas, power, cable, or telephone service account on your credit reports while they're in good standing. There are some exceptions. I've seen credit reports with accounts from NICOR (a gas provider in Illinois) reporting month after month just like any other loan. Most of the time if you see these types of accounts on a credit report it's because they've been sent to collections and the collector is reporting it.

INSURANCE PAYMENTS

Almost all insurance companies will allow you to pay your insurance premium in installments. I'm quite certain most people would consider that a form of extending credit, and I'd agree with them. However, insurance companies do not report the installment payments to the credit reporting agencies. If you don't pay them, they'll just cancel your coverage. And of course, driving without insurance is illegal. Talk about the ultimate leverage over their borrowers!

RENTAL PAYMENTS

Because most landlords don't have accounts with the credit reporting agencies, many are unable to report your rental payment history. And until recently, you'd rarely, if ever, see your rental payments on your credit report even if you lived in an apartment complex with hundreds or thousands of units. However, even though some rental payments are now being included regularly in credit report updates, Experian is the only credit bureau where rental payments may show up. Of course, if you default on your lease they'll turn it over to a collection agency, and you'll see that on your credit reports lickety-split.

CHAPTER 3

Negative Items & Credit Reporting Errors

So, you've made some credit mistakes. With over 35 percent of the population scoring below 650 on the FICO scoring scale, you're certainly not alone. But now that you've made the mistakes, how long are you going to have to live with them?

NEGATIVE ITEMS

Each and every negative item has a reportable statute of limitations. That means the credit bureaus can legally report it for some period of time before it must be removed. The general consensus is seven years for the credit reporting of negative items. And while that's correct for many negative credit items, it's not always right and certainly not always that simple.

Bankruptcy

This one has possibly the most confusing statute of limitations, so let's get it out of the way first. Chapter 7 bankruptcies (liquidation of all statutorily dischargeable debts) can remain on your credit files for ten years from the date filed. Chapter 13 bank-ruptcies (wage earner programs where you're still making pay-ments to the trustee) can remain on file for seven years **from the discharge date**. This is important because most people believe Chapter 13s have to be removed seven years from the filing date, which is incorrect. It normally takes three to five years for a Chapter 13 to discharge. That's when the seven years begin. The cap on all bankruptcies is ten years, so most Chapter 13s remain on file for a full ten years, just like Chapter 7s.

Tax Liens
This one has the longest statute of limitations and must be broken down into three categories: released, unpaid, and withdrawn.

- **Released Tax Liens**: Released liens can remain on file for seven years from the date released. This includes liens that have been settled for less than you really owe.
- **Unpaid Tax Liens**: Sit down. Unpaid tax liens can remain on your credit file indefinitely. That's the bad news. Now the good news . . .
- **Paid and Withdrawn Tax Liens**: Paid tax liens normally stay on file for seven years, but the IRS just announced that they will withdraw the lien if it is paid in full AND the taxpayer requests a withdrawal. The credit bureaus do not report withdrawn tax liens, so they will come off your files almost immediately if you get them withdrawn.

Defaulted Government-Guaranteed Student Loans
Interestingly, the Fair Credit Reporting Act doesn't govern the amount of time defaulted student loans can remain on your credit reports. The amount of time is actually governed by the Higher Education Act instead. Defaulted student loans can

remain on your credit reports for seven years from the date they are paid, seven years from the date they were first reported, or seven years from the date the loan re-defaults. The point you should take away from this: pay your student loans!

The Seven-Year Club

The following items can remain on your credit files for seven years:

- **Delinquent Child-Support Obligations**
- **Judgments**: Seven years from the filing date whether satisfied or not
- **Collections**: Seven years from date of default with the **original** creditor, not seven years from when the collection agency buys or is consigned the debt
- **Charge-Offs**: Seven years from the date of the original terminal delinquency
- **Settlements**: Seven years from the date of the original terminal delinquency
- **Repossessions and Foreclosures**: Seven years from the date of the original terminal delinquency
- **Late Payments**: Seven years from the date of occurrence

You'll notice that I use the term "terminal delinquency" several times above. The seven-year period actually begins 180 days *after* the original delinquency that leads to a collection, charge-off, or similarly negative action. So, technically these items remain on your credit file for seven and a half years from the date of the last delinquency that precedes the terminal delinquency.

The Forever Club

If your credit report is being accessed for a loan of $150,000 or more, then none of the seven- and ten-year rules are binding.

That means the credit bureaus *could* maintain this negative stuff permanently, but only for credit reports where you've applied for a higher dollar loan. They also have an exemption for credit reports sold for employment screening where the job is expected to pay $75,000 or more. Thankfully, the credit bureaus choose to use the seven- and ten-year guidelines regardless.

You Don't Have to Do Anything, Unless . . .

Other than the tax lien withdrawal process described above, the consumer doesn't have to do anything in order to have negative credit information removed on or before the expiration of the applicable statute of limitations. The process of removing negative information is on autopilot and based on a passive date trigger or "purge from" date.

Now, since it's based on a trigger date, there is room for error in the cases of incorrect credit reporting. If the bank says you defaulted in 2005 and you really defaulted in 2004, then the credit bureaus are going to use the 2005 date. Then it's up to you to argue with (or sue) the lender and the credit bureaus to get the dates correct.

Re-Aging

If you've never heard of this term, let's hope you never do. Re-aging is the illegal process of changing the "purge from" date so the credit reporting extends past the allowable period of time. This is not common, but when it's done, it's usually a collection agency or debt buyer who is breaking the rules. It's a clear violation of the Fair Debt Collection Practices Act and the Fair Credit Reporting Act, but the debtor has to know it has happened and press the issue to protect his or her rights.

HOW TO CORRECT CREDIT REPORT ERRORS

Correcting errors in your credit reports seems like it would be an easy task. You get copies of your reports, you review them for accuracy, and if you find something wrong you file disputes with the credit bureaus to have them corrected. Simple, right? Unfortunately it's not as simple as I just suggested, but following these tips will help to ease the pain:

Make Sure It's Really an Error

Keep in mind that credit reports are not real-time, which means the balances on your accounts are going to be from the previous month's statement. And if you just wrote a check a few days ago to pay off a collection or a loan, that's not going to be reflected on your credit reports yet. So, the question is, "is it really an error?" Clearly a balance that isn't your true current balance can be a problem, but since the credit reporting system isn't, has never been, and likely will never be a real-time system, you have to reset your expectations as to what is accurate and what is inaccurate. You can certainly dispute the balance as inaccurate, but it would have likely been updated in the next few days or weeks anyway.

Burn the Candle at Both Ends

The credit bureaus don't generally get involved in disputes between you and your creditors. They're simply warehouses that store information sent to them by their data furnishers (your creditors and collectors seeking payment from you). When you send them a dispute, they will send notification of that dispute to the data furnisher. This is the standard protocol for all disputes unless you're disputing a public record.

The credit bureaus generally will send the creditor/collector an automated form called an ACDV (Automated Consumer Dispute Verification) via a web-based system called e-OSCAR (Online Solution for Complete and Accurate Reporting). There is very little human involvement, and the credit bureaus will simply report what the data furnisher tells them to report in response to the dispute. This is called "parroting."

If your disputed item comes back as "verified as accurate," then you really should contact the creditor directly and take up the argument with them. There's no sense in re-disputing the item over and over through the credit bureaus, and eventually they'll consider repeats as being "frivolous," which then allows them to ignore your disputes. In fact, I'd suggest directly contacting the creditor right out of the gate.

Think about Going Old-School

If you file an online dispute from a credit report you claimed at AnnualCreditReport.com, then the bureaus (a) have forty-five days to complete their investigation versus thirty days and (b) only give you a list of preselected dispute reasons, which may or may not exactly match up with your dispute. If your dispute is atypical, then I'd suggest that you type up a letter and mail it to the bureaus. If your dispute is garden-variety ("not my account" or "balance paid in full"), then go ahead and file it online.

Be Vigilant

If you know for a fact that what's being reported is wrong *and* that error is significant to the point that it's costing you money, or worse, a job, you should not simply live with it for seven to ten years. The challenge you face is, unlike our legal system, you're guilty until someone else tells the credit bureaus that you're not. The bureaus will never take your word over one of their revenue-generating data buyers/data furnishers. And while the bureaus and I don't share pleasantries very often, I can't blame them. According to their trade association, the CDIA, about 30 percent of the disputes are submitted by credit repair organizations. That equals millions of disputes each year that may not be real disputes, but instead are simply attempts to get accurate but negative data removed early. Point being, if you really want to get your credit files corrected and the standard process isn't working for you, then you might have to escalate your efforts into the legal environment to get it corrected.

CHAPTER 4

Credit Reports: They're Not Just for Lenders

It's commonly known and generally accepted that banks, credit card issuers, auto lenders, credit unions, and finance companies see your credit reports when you apply for a credit benefit. And, depending on your relationship with your lender, many of them can pull your credit reports and scores as often as they want as part of their ongoing account management practices. But what many people don't realize is that other entities have the ability to see your credit reports and do so enjoying the protection of the Fair Credit Reporting Act.

Collectors

Were you aware that collection agencies are allowed to pull, score, and review your credit reports? And they're allowed to do so without your permission as long as they're trying to collect a debt from you. That's right, a collection agency can pull your credit reports without you knowing or giving permission.

So, what are they looking for? Simple, they're looking for *you*. That's right, your credit report likely contains your current address, which is golden to debt collectors because they can send you collection notices and even have you served if they choose to sue you for the debt. Further, they can also see if you have open credit cards with available credit, and thus the ability to charge the payment for the collection.

Employers

We already know that employers can review your credit reports, in most states, as part of their employment screening processes. However, they have to disclose to you, in writing, before they access your credit. Employers are looking for signs of irresponsibility and a heavy burden of debt, which might tempt your evil side. And, of course, credit scores are not provided to employers along with employment screening credit reports. I'll go into more depth on this topic as we take a look at a number of ever-present, and often misleading, FICO score myths and debunk them in Chapter 9: *Credit Score Myths: Setting the Record Straight.*

Insurance Companies

That's right, insurance companies can review your credit as part of their underwriting processes. However, some states are trying to eliminate the practice or otherwise limit what can be used from your credit report to determine your insurance risk. In addition to your credit report, insurance companies can also use your insurance credit score not only to determine your risk of filing a claim, but also as a way to measure how profitable you'd be as a customer.

So is the use of insurance credit scoring valuable to insurance companies? In a word, absolutely. In fact, according to Lamont Boyd, director of FICO's insurance market, "Most states understand the value of credit-based insurance scoring to the insurance industry and to consumers alike, allowing for more accurate underwriting and pricing decisions for new applications and existing policies." What he's saying is simple: insurance scoring, which is based in part on your credit report, allows insurance companies to properly price policies based on risk, which is great for consumers who have good credit because they'll generally pay less than consumers with bad credit. And good news: insurance inquiries don't negatively impact your FICO scores.

Utility Companies

Have you ever wondered how a utility provider determines whether or not they're going to assess a deposit on a new account? You guessed it; it's based in part on your credit report and your utility credit score. The good news is that if you've got good credit, it's unlikely you'll have to pay a deposit for utilities. The best news is that utility inquiries don't count in your FICO credit scores.

Landlords

Landlords also have the ability to review your credit reports before they hand over the keys. You probably already knew that. And some states can review your credit prior to granting a professional license, such as one for a mortgage broker or a general contractor. It's tough to escape the influence of your credit on your ability to do just about anything. This is why it's always important to maintain solid credit and solid credit scores. They're important for many reasons that have nothing to do with interest rates and loan approvals.

CHAPTER 5

Myth Busting, Credit Report–Style

Here are four of the most commonly misrepresented "facts" about credit reporting:

THE CREDIT REPORTING AGENCIES
SHARE INFORMATION WITH EACH OTHER

The credit reporting agencies are competitors, which means they are trying to steal business from each other. They all maintain independent databases full of credit, collection, and public record information. The databases are not linked to each other, meaning they do not share information about your loans, collections, credit scores, or public records with each other. They do, however, share fraud alerts, so if you add a fraud alert to one of your credit reports, then they will share it with the other reporting agencies. Of course, they're forced to do this by federal law.

YOUR CREDIT REPORTS ARE UPDATED
IN REAL TIME

As mentioned in Chapter 3, your credit reports are not updated as you make payments and charge items. The lenders whom you do business with only update your account with the credit bureaus once per month, not multiple times per month. This means when you swipe your card at a gas station or grocery store, the merchant knows about it and the card issuer knows about it because they had to approve the transaction, but it can take the credit bureaus up to a month to know about it. If you look at your credit reports, the data at any given time is about thirty days old. What this means is any credit scores that are calculated using this information will be based on data that isn't real-time.

THE CREDIT REPORTING AGENCIES DETERMINE
WHAT COUNTS IN YOUR FICO SCORE

Despite the fact that the credit reporting agencies *do* calculate and then sell your FICO scores to lenders, they do not control what is considered and they do not control how much certain things count. The only influence they have over your FICO score is the data they have in their system connected to you, and that's where it ends. FICO is fully responsible for the design and development of their own scoring system. This means the inner workings of the model, including what counts and how much, is proprietary. Not only do consumers not know exactly how the scoring system works, neither do the credit bureaus.

THE CREDIT REPORT AGENCIES CAN NEVER
REPORT NEGATIVE ITEMS LONGER THAN
SEVEN TO TEN YEARS

As I previously discussed, there is actually a little-known exclusion to the "seven- to ten-year" rule for reporting negative credit information. The Fair Credit Reporting Act actually allows the credit bureaus to report negative information longer than seven to ten years under the following application conditions:

- If it's for a credit transaction that involves an amount greater than $150,000
- If it's for a life insurance policy with a face value greater than $150,000
- If it's for employment purposes and the salary is going to be greater than $75,000

So while some of you may not like the credit reporting agencies, I think we have to be honest about the fact that they are actually taking it easy on many of us. How many mortgage loans exceed $150,000, and how many of your jobs pay more than $75,000? In every single one of those cases, they *could* have gotten an exemption to the seven to ten year rule when compiling your credit report. That means your mortgage lender and your employer could have seen some negative information that is older than seven to ten years.

COUPLES AND CREDIT REPORTS: MORE MYTH BUSTING

Every year in honor of the annual Valentine's Day festivities, an average of 200,000 couples get engaged. That's roughly 10 percent of the engagements that are projected to occur this year in the United States. And while most of these couples will soon tie the proverbial knot and profess to live as one until "death do us part," the mechanics of the credit system don't necessarily follow those rules. In fact, there are a fair number of myths regarding couples and their credit. Here are a few of the most common:

Your Credit Reports Merge with Those of Your New Spouse

This is probably the most common of the "couples and credit" myths. The credit reporting system in this country maintains records on individual consumers, not on households or couples. This means even though you are married, your credit reports do not magically merge with those of your new spouse.

The only time credit reports are merged is in the mortgage environment, when you apply jointly for a home loan. The lender will use the services of what's referred to as a "mortgage reporting company," who will pull all three of your credit reports and all three of your spouse's credit reports, and then combine them into one large joint credit report. The final product is called a Residential Mortgage Credit Report or RMCR. It gives the impression that you and your spouse have fully integrated credit reports, but it is simply a cosmetic exercise.

Your Credit *Scores* Merge with Those of Your New Spouse

This is probably the second most common couples-related credit myth, partially because of the RMCR process I described above. Credit scores, like credit reports, do not merge when you get married. In fact, credit scores aren't even a permanent part of your credit reports, which is why the free annual credit report law doesn't mandate a free credit score.

Credit scores are calculated on individual credit reports and then delivered with that report to the lender or whoever else is buying the report. If credit reports were merged and maintained by the credit bureaus, then joint credit scores could be easily calculated. But since reports are not maintained jointly . . . no joint credit scores.

You Are Required to Apply Jointly for Credit with Your New Spouse

Absolutely not true. There is no law or lender requirement that forces spouses to apply jointly for credit simply because they're a couple. Applying jointly for credit is a choice and it can work for you, or it can work against you.

When you apply jointly for any sort of credit (cards, auto loan, mortgage), the lender is now allowed to hold both of you liable for the payments. And since both of you are now liable for the debt, the lender can—and probably will—report the account to both of your credit reports. This means if payments are made on time and the account is managed properly, then your credit and your spouse's credit reports and credit scores will benefit.

If, however, the account is managed poorly, that will also show up on both of your credit reports, and you will both suffer. If the account goes to some sort of terminal level of delinquency, such as a collection, then both of you will be hounded for the payments. And finally, if the lender or collection attorney chooses to sue you for the amount of the debt, then both of you may find yourselves on the wrong side of the lawsuit.

You Are Liable for Your New Spouse's Debt

This isn't entirely wrong, but it's certainly not entirely right, either. If you cosign or apply jointly for credit, then it's a done deal . . . you're liable. But if you don't cosign or jointly apply for credit, then it's likely that you are not liable for his or her debt. For example, if you're simply added to a credit card account as what's called an "authorized user," then you're not contractually liable for the debt.

The likely exception to that rule occurs if you live in one of the community property states. At the time this book went to print, the states were California, Louisiana, Alaska, Arizona, Idaho, Nevada, New Mexico, Texas, Washington, and Wisconsin. If the debt was incurred while living in those states, a creditor (and therefore a collector) can make the argument that even though an individual incurred the debt, both parties benefitted and thus both parties are liable for payment. This is why after a death or a divorce, collectors attempt to collect from the surviving spouses.

A Divorce Decree Releases Me from Liability

I hate to bring this up, but the rate of divorce filings is half of the rate of marriages. What this means is a whole lot of couples get divorced every year and most of them have joint debts, which need to be somehow separated. The problem is that while your divorce attorney is probably very smart when it comes to divorces, he or she isn't a financial counselor and won't spend time advising you on how best to separate liabilities.

The court can assign payment responsibilities to one spouse or the other, but that doesn't change the terms of the original lender contract signed by the two spouses. And since the lender isn't present at your divorce proceedings, and isn't a party to your agreement, they are not bound by it. If you have joint credit cards before your divorce, you still have joint credit cards after it.

This is problematic because if the payments are missed they will show up on both spouses' credit reports and can damage both sets of credit scores. And trust me, arguing that "my ex-husband is supposed to pay that" isn't going to work. Any division of credit liabilities must be done in such a way that the lender acknowledges the changes. This means you'll have to make the lender a party to any "legal" division of joint credit liabilities, and I can tell you that this is next to impossible. It's easier to sell off assets and close credit card accounts.

PART II

Credit Scores

CHAPTER 6

Credit Scores: Three Is the Magic Number

Each of the three credit reporting agencies house and maintain more than 200 million consumer credit files. The vast majority of those credit files are what's referred to as "scoreable." This means they meet certain minimum criteria set forth by the credit score developers in order to support the calculation of a credit score.

For example, in order for you to have a FICO score, your credit file must have at least one undisputed trade line (account) that is older than six months, one undisputed trade line that has been updated in the last six months, and no indication on your credit file that you are deceased.

One account can satisfy the first two criteria. So, if you opened a Discover credit card five years ago and it was just updated in your credit file last month (and you're alive), then your credit file will be scoreable under the FICO system.

The minimum scoring criteria for VantageScore is very different. In order to qualify for a VantageScore, the consumer's credit file must have at least one account that has had some sort of activity in the past two years.

And while most of us focus on FICO as the dominant credit score on the market, with VantageScore providing their main competition in the "credit bureau score" arena, that's hardly where it ends.

HOW MANY CREDIT SCORES DO YOU HAVE?

In fact, you've got so many more scores that if I tried to name all of them, and explain what each of them do, your head would spin and I'd run out of paper. But because I never shy away from a credit-related challenge, here's an abbreviated version:

FICO

FICO is not only a score type, but also a brand. It's kind of like saying "Coke," which is an actual soft drink and also a brand representing a long list of soft drinks. FICO builds a large variety of scoring systems, but we're generally focused on their core product: their credit bureau–based risk scores, or "FICO" scores.

In addition, FICO also builds bankruptcy scores, revenue scores, industry-specific variations of their FICO credit risk scores, attritions scores, response scores, transactions scores, medical adherence scores, collection scores, behavior scores, application scores, small business risk scores, fraud scores, insurance risk scores . . . and the list goes on and on.

All of these scores have various "generations" (or versions) that may still be available to lenders and other industries. The raw number of score options is truly mind-boggling. According to Craig Watts from FICO, "By our count, US lenders and other businesses used roughly four billion FICO scores last year that were calculated from precisely the same scoring models used to calculate the scores that myFICO.com sells." To put that in perspective, that's only one version of their FICO risk score and *not* all of those other above-mentioned scores.

VantageScore

VantageScore Solutions builds a credit bureau–based risk score and is currently on version 2.0 of that scoring system. They do not build other types of scores, but their core product, the VantageScore, is gaining some market share.

Equifax, Experian, and TransUnion

All three of the credit reporting agencies have a long history of developing scoring systems. Collectively they build risk scores, collection and recovery scores, insurance scores, bankruptcy scores, and many more.

Lenders, Insurance Companies, and Utility Providers

Most large lenders, insurance companies, and utility providers use credit scoring systems. And many of them are homegrown, meaning they were custom-built for use by one company. Point being, they're each going to have their own suite of scoring models, which multiplies the total number under which you could be scored.

So now that you know this, how many scores do you have? The answer is simple . . . you don't know. What we do know is that you can be scored under each of the scoring systems I mentioned, which likely brings the number into the hundreds.

When I was working for FICO, one of my job functions was to go out and speak about credit scoring at various credit industry–related events. I was almost always the least popular guy in the room because of my subject matter. This was true on all but one occasion, when a credit card risk manager from one of the mega banks joined me as a panelist for a score discussion. He told the crowd that his bank scored their customers, on average, over sixty times each year using a variety of different types of scores. For the first time in a long time, I was no longer the least popular guy in the room.

Keep in mind that this was one bank, not all banks. Now multiply his number of sixty by the number of credit cards in your wallet. That will give you a better indication of just how often you're being scored each year. For those of you who think you understand credit scoring, you're just scratching the surface. So the next time you hear someone telling you that "your score is X," you'll know better.

HOW TO NAVIGATE THE THREE CREDIT SCORE SYSTEM

Each of us has three credit reports housed by the three major credit reporting agencies: Experian, Equifax, and TransUnion. And for most of us, those three credit files are scoreable, as I explained in the previous section.

And while it's a fact that none of us have just three credit scores, it is also a fact that most lenders will make decisions using just one of our credit bureau risk scores. This means when you apply for a credit card or an auto loan, the lender is going to buy one of your three credit reports and one of your three FICO scores or, less frequently, one of your three VantageScores. The only exception to that "one report, one loan" rule is the mortgage environment, where the lender will almost always pull all three of your credit reports, all three of your FICO scores, and then base their decision on your middle score.

How Widely Your Scores Can Range

Each of your credit scores are going to be different, primarily because the information in our credit files is never 100 percent identical. And because of the common lending practice of only pulling one credit score, it's almost a guarantee that lenders are going to see different numbers for us depending on which of our three credit reports they happen to purchase.

For example, my FICO scores vary by twenty-four points from my highest score to my lowest. My highest score is based on my Equifax data, and my lowest is based on my TransUnion data. This means if I applied for any loan outside of a mortgage and the lender pulled my TransUnion credit report, they'd see my lowest FICO score. If that "lowest" score fell below the lender's risk threshold, I could be denied the loan, or approved but with less advantageous terms.

My example isn't a good one because my scores are all pretty good, so I'd likely still get approved even if the lender saw my lowest score. But getting the lender's best deal isn't a slam dunk for consumers who either (a) have a larger variance between their scores, or (b) have three marginal scores to begin with. In fact, I fielded a question two weeks ago from a guy whose highest FICO score was 748, which is very strong. The problem is that his lowest FICO score was 658, a full ninety points off from his high score. A 658, as you probably already know, is not very good and is right on the borderline of being considered "subprime."

The gentleman had a collection on one of his credit reports that wasn't being reported to his other two credit reports. This isn't a terribly uncommon scenario, as reporting to all three credit bureaus isn't mandatory under any federal or state laws. What this does, however, is place any consumer in a position where they're rolling the dice each time they apply for a loan because they don't know (a) what their three scores are, (b) what credit report is going to be scored the highest, and (c) what credit report and score their lenders are going to see.

The two examples I highlighted above (mine and the guy with the collection) are both what I would define as being bookend examples. It's been my experience that most consumers fall in between those bookends. So the question is how can we ensure that we're putting our best foot forward when we apply for loans? Here are some things to keep in mind before you apply for a loan.

1. You Can't Force Your Lender to Pull One Credit Report over Another   Lenders have what are referred to as "credit bureau preference tables" and they use those tables to decide which of your three credit reports they're going to pull, based on where you live. Now, you *can* shop around and ask lenders which credit report they pull for consumers living in your local area, and if you can find a lender who uses the same credit bureau where you've got your highest score, BINGO! I call that "strategic shopping," and it takes shopping around for the best interest rate to a different level.

2. You Can't Bring Your Credit Report and Score with You to the Lender   Lenders will want to pull the report and score on their own so that it can be fed into their automated underwriting system. There was also a pretty funny story about a guy in Butte, Montana, a few years ago who used Photoshop to change information on his credit report. He walked out with an auto loan, but was arrested shortly after for loan fraud.

3. Auto Dealers Will Likely Pull Your Credit Report and Then Shop Your Loan Around to Other Lenders   Those other lenders will also want to pull your credit report. This practice is very common, and it can lead to lenders seeing different scores depending on where they've decided to buy your credit report and score. If you know of a local lender in your area who uses the credit report where you've got your best score, it's not a bad idea to apply for the loan with them and "take the financing" with you to the dealership, meaning that you've been pre-approved by another lender before you started your car shopping. That's your ace in the hole. If they can beat that rate with another deal, then take the better deal. Again, this is strategic shopping.

4. Shelve Your Credit Cards for One Full Cycle   The way the credit reporting system is set up, the balances on your credit cards are updated only once a month and it's based on your previous month's statement. If you pay your cards in full each month, your credit reports are still not reflecting the $0 balance because it's likely that you used them again during the following month. If possible, pay them off in full and leave your cards in your wallet until you've closed on your new loan. This ensures the lowest possible "utilization percentage." (See Chapter 10 for a full explanation of utilization percentages, and why having the right one is good for your score.) This strategy will work with all three credit reports and scores, not just one of them.

NOTE: As mentioned earlier, we all have a fourth credit report housed by Innovis Data Solutions, but that particular credit report is not scoreable under the FICO or VantageScore systems. Further, Innovis doesn't currently sell credit reports to lenders for use in underwriting.

CHAPTER 7

FICO Score Distribution:
A "Flattening of the Curve"

About 35 percent of US consumers now have FICO scores under 650. Statisticians call it a "flattening of the curve," and it represents the movement of a population into the tails of a distribution. OK, no more statistics mumbo jumbo, I promise. Let's just say that for the first time since the installation of the FICO credit bureau–based scoring system in 1989, 35 percent of the population is now scoring below 650.

Each of the three credit bureaus maintain between 200 and 250 million credit file records, which means between 70 and 87.5 million consumers are now scoring below 650. To make matters even worse, 25.5 percent of them (or roughly 51 million people) are scoring below 600. For these folks, "credit" is now as distant to them as, say, retirement. It just isn't going to happen any time soon.

That 650 score break is meaningful because in today's financial services environment, many lenders and insurance companies consider the +/− 650 point to be the dividing line between prime and subprime. What this means is more consumers are going to be denied or adversely approved (when you're approved, but with less than favorable rates or terms). And if someone is waiting for the US consumer to spend us back into a fully functioning and healthy economy, the push won't come from those folks.

There are some who have argued that this drop in FICO scores is actually healthy and is being caused by our insatiable appetite for things that require us to get into too much debt. This is simply not true. For any of you who know anything about FICO scoring, you know that you don't end up with scores below 650 (and well below 650 in most cases) because of secured and/or unsecured debt.

No, the real reason you end up "down there" is because of negative information hitting your credit files. The debt contributes to really low scores, but it doesn't cause really low scores. What this FICO data reflects is an extraordinary number of consumers who now have foreclosures, settlements, charge-offs, collections, bankruptcies, liens, judgments, late payments, and repossessions on their credit reports, and much lower scores as a result.

What makes this news even more disturbing is the fact that the aforementioned negative items remain on your credit reports for between seven and ten years. This means scores that are trending lower will continue to do so for many years to come and will stymie any sort of consumer-based economic recovery. Add to that an unemployment rate of 10 percent and an "underemployment" rate (employed but not making what you were making) that's much higher, and it spells bad news.

The lone bright spot from the FICO data is that negative information does eventually have to be removed from your credit files. It can't persist indefinitely. And as it ages, it loses negative value, which means if you do nothing other than exist, your scores will improve organically over time. It's just going to make loans, credit cards, and insurance more expensive for the next few years.

This FICO score data isn't bad news for everyone. And, as I always say, "when it gets dark outside, the rats and roaches come out to play." If you assume that consumers won't subject themselves to credit "prohibition" for the next seven to ten years, you have to conclude that they will be doing credit-based business with someone. And this means super subprime lenders such as pawn shops, title lenders, and payday lenders will be there to mop up their fair share of the demand. These are obviously some pretty bad options that should be used only if you are truly desperate for short-term funds.

So, digest this FICO data and then throw it out, because regardless of why there are now 70 million consumers with FICO <650, what really matters is what *your* FICO scores are. And happily, FICO scoring is a very individual measurement based on what you've done lately rather than what we've all done lately. Thank goodness for that!

CHAPTER 8

Credit Score Confusion: What Are You Buying?

On July 19, 2011, the newly formed Consumer Financial Protection Bureau submitted a report to Congress that studied the credit-scoring marketplace. The goal of their study was to inventory the credit scores marketed to consumers as opposed to those credit scores sold to lenders, and then identify any areas where consumers could possibly be "harmed" by the practice. The study revealed what many of us already know, which is that the consumer market is flooded with credit scores that have little or no influence on your ability to get credit.

The selling of credit-related products and services to you and me has become a big business . . . a really big business. The market for these products and services started evolving in the very late 1990s (thanks to the Internet) and blew up in the middle part of this decade. Now we have a dozen or so companies who dominate the airwaves with advertisements for credit scores and credit monitoring services. Have you ever wondered why?

CREDIT REPORTS ARE FREE . . . FOR A CREDIT BUREAU, ANYWAY

Credit reports have almost no "cost of goods," which means they cost practically nothing to produce. It's not like they require metal, glass, wiring, wood, machinery, or rubber to create. And there's no labor to deliver them. It's 100 percent automated. The credit reporting agencies don't have to go pay someone for a credit report in order to resell it to you. They already own the data, and new data is continually being given to them for free by their network of data furnishers (lenders and collection agencies).

"EDUCATIONAL" CREDIT SCORING MODELS ARE CHEAP TO BUILD

Building a credit-scoring model (one that is not going to be sold to lenders) can be done by a decent credit score developer during his lunch break, which means it costs basically nothing to build. Yet you can run credit data through that model hundreds of thousands of times each day and produce a score that can be called a "credit score" in marketing advertisements. And since consumers aren't hyper-sophisticated on the topic of credit scores, it's not a surprise that they really believe their "credit score" is, in fact, their legitimate credit score.

This confusion was identified by the Consumer Financial Protection Bureau (CFPB) as one of the areas where consumers could be harmed by industry practices. "A consumer, unaware of the variety of credit scores available in the marketplace, may purchase a score believing it to be his or her "true" (or only) credit score, when in fact there is no such single score."

In my mind, consumers would also probably be a little more than irritated if/when they found out that what they're paying for isn't really what lenders are seeing. The CFPB agreed, stating that "the consumer would have spent money on a score or subscribed to a credit monitoring service that he or she otherwise might not have purchased. Believing he or she purchased a FICO score may lead to dissatisfaction upon learning otherwise."

THE MOST SUBSTANTIAL PROBLEM WITH "EDUCATIONAL" CREDIT SCORES

The CFPB identified what they believed to be the most substantial problem with buying an educational score as being misrepresentation. Not misrepresentation in marketing language, but a misrepresentation of the consumer's actual credit risk. "The most substantial harm would likely result if, after purchasing a score, a consumer has a different impression of his or her creditworthiness than a lender would."

Essentially what this means is if you buy a score online somewhere and that score tells you that you're a 750, you might walk into a lender's office with the expectation of being treated like someone with FICO 750. However, if the lender pulls your legitimate FICO score and sees a 698, then you're not going to be treated like a 750. That is a scenario that has no winners. The consumer is either embarrassed or might even think the lender is being dishonest.

This can cut both ways. You get your score online and think you're a 698, but your lender pulls your FICO score and sees a 750. In that case the news you'll receive from the lender, hopefully, will be great: "John, you've been approved at our best rate." Still, this better outcome is suboptimal, because you might be seeking credit from a subprime lender who can't match a mainstream bank's best offers.

WHY DON'T THEY ALL SELL FICO SCORES?

This is a reasonable question with a complicated answer. First off, it takes two to tango. Not only does FICO have to agree to have their core product distributed by a third party, but that third party has to want to distribute FICO scores. Experian doesn't want to allow the distribution of FICO scores (based on Experian credit report data) to consumers and canceled an agreement allowing FICO to do so in February 2009. TransUnion and Equifax still allow FICO to sell FICO scores to consumers based on their data, but they also both sell non-FICO scores to consumers.

Right now the credit reporting agencies seem like they're more interested in FICO going away than helping to further brand their own scores as the industry standard. It's not hard to understand why. Each time a FICO score is calculated, the company is paid a royalty, and deservedly so. Each time a non-FICO score is calculated, the company is not paid a royalty. See where I'm headed?

That brings us back to the CFPB report on credit scoring. The report found that "when a consumer purchases a credit score from a CRA (credit reporting agency), he or she will often receive a score that will not be the same score used by a lender to evaluate the consumer's creditworthiness."

What's the take-away? It's that we as buyers need to be aware that what we're buying isn't what Bank of America, Chase, and Wells Fargo are buying when we're applying for loans. As long as you are comfortable knowing that, then no harm, no foul, and the CFPB report isn't meaningful to you. However, if you want the same exact score "brand" your lenders are likely using, then your options are limited to FICO's consumer website, myFICO.com. But even then, it's probably not the same FICO score that your lender is using.

CHAPTER 9

Credit Score Myths: Setting
the Record Straight

Before we get this party started, let's review the difference
between two essential credit-related terms:

1. **Credit File**. A credit file is a collection of information housed at one or more of the credit reporting
   agencies. This information is generally made up of
   third-party collections, some public records, iden-
   tification information, inquiries, and your accounts.
   When it is requested, by a lender for example, it is
   delivered in the form of a credit report.
2. **Credit Score**. A credit score is the distillation of
   much of the information in your credit report to
   a three-digit number, which is designed to predict
   whether or not you'll go ninety days past due on any
   credit obligation in the next twenty-four months.
   The most commonly used credit score is the FICO
   score. Scores are **not** a permanent part of your credit

file, and they do not persist in the credit bureau's databases. They are calculated on a one-off basis, delivered, and then forgotten. Credit scores are sold as ancillary products along with credit reports, kind of like buying floor mats with a car.

Now that we've gotten that straight, we'll move on.

THE USE OF CREDIT SCORES FOR EMPLOYMENT SCREENING: TIME TO SET THE RECORD STRAIGHT

According to section 604 of the Fair Credit Reporting Act, it is perfectly legal for any of the credit reporting agencies to furnish a credit report for the purposes of employment screening. Some states have made it illegal, but it's still perfectly legal in most states thanks to federal law. Your overt permission must be given in order for a prospective employer (or current employer) to access your credit report, which is different from a lender pulling your credit report, where no overt permission is required.

The credit reporting agencies, the root source of credit reports for employment screening, do not provide the same type of credit report to employers as they provide to lenders, insurance companies, landlords, or utility providers. It is a specifically designed version only for use by employers or employee-screening companies. This is important because credit *scores* are **not** provided with those employment-specific reports. Read that again, please.

Nonetheless, the terms credit *report* and credit *score* are used too interchangeably, and many people have come to believe that they are the same thing. And because of that, many people believe that credit *scores* play some role in whether or not you will get or keep a job. This, of course, is not true and it is only the credit *report* that might play that role, but only with your permission.

Greg Fisher from CreditScoring.com created a video collage of many media outlets, a mistaken Equifax executive, and even a FICO advertisement all claiming that employers use scores. This is, of course, contributing to the life of a myth that just won't die. The video can be found on YouTube at http://bit.ly/cs-video, in case you want to take a look. It's well worth eight minutes of your life, trust me.

All of the credit reporting agencies have gone on record time and time again stating that they do not provide credit scores to employers. The Consumer Data Industry Association (CDIA), the trade organization of the credit reporting agencies, has done the same. In fact, according to Stuart Pratt, president of the CDIA, "None of the credit reporting agencies sell credit scores to employers, so credit scores don't influence any sort of employment decision." Kirsten Snyder, public relations manager at Experian, sent me a list of what is *not* delivered to employers. "Credit score" is on that list. So those of you who believe, suspect, or insist that a bad credit score will cost you a job, take comfort in the fact that it simply is untrue, despite what many seem to believe.

FICO SCORE MYTHS DEBUNKED

FICO scores have been around since 1989, but they weren't thrust into the public eye until the mid 1990s, when Fannie Mae and Freddie Mac endorsed their use in the mortgage environment. And by "endorsed" I mean "forced." Mortgage lenders had until the late '90s to fully implement FICO scoring into their underwriting processes. I was at FICO when this happened and one of my jobs was to crisscross the country speaking at mortgage broker and banker events, teaching these really angry people about the new tool that just got shoved down their throats. Talk about being the least popular guy in the room.

Fannie Mae and Freddie Mac are what are referred to as Government Sponsored Enterprises, or GSEs, and this GSE "endorsement" also meant a whole lot of public scrutiny of a tool that had always remained a secret to consumers, albeit unintentionally. I mean, if you don't sell something directly to consumers, then why would consumers know about it? No, FICO's entry into the mortgage market meant more press, more attention, more criticism, more work for me, and a whole lot of incorrect information being passed off as the truth.

So, here is a list of a few FICO score myths that I have run into over the past twelve years, and the subsequent debunking. There are certainly many more, but these are some of the most common.

Myth #1: FICO Scores Consider Income

This is incorrect. The FICO scores that we're all familiar with are credit bureau–based scoring models. That means they only consider information on your credit reports. And guess what? Your income is not on your credit reports. There are models that consider income, as listed on your credit applications, but these are not the FICO scores that we all know and love.

Bottom line: Income is a measurement of capacity (whether or not you can afford your payment) not creditworthiness (whether or not you'll choose to make your payment.)

Myth #2: Closing a Credit Card Will Improve Your FICO Scores

This is incorrect. It does seem to be common sense, though; less available credit should mean you can't get into as much credit card debt and therefore you're a better credit risk, right? The problem with that hypothesis is that it's incorrect. And thankfully, credit score development isn't a commonsense exercise. The empirical evidence shows, and has shown for over two decades, that having a lot of "open to buy" (unused) credit limits equates to better credit risk. This is commonly referred to as "revolving utilization," the percentage of your credit limits that you're currently using. Closing cards can actually increase this utilization percentage and lower your scores.

There's a secondary myth to this one that says keeping your utilization percentage at or below 30 percent is the best for your score. That's also incorrect. Nothing magical happens at 30 percent. It's better than 40 percent, but not as good as 20 percent. In fact, according to FICO, consumers who have scores above 760 have an average utilization percentage of just 7 percent.

Bottom line: Shoot for lowering your balances to $0 if you can, but if you can't, get them as low as you can and your FICO scores will benefit. NOTE: This only applies to credit cards, not installment loans.

Myth #3: Closing a Card Causes You to Lose the "Age" Benefit of That Account.

This is incorrect. One of the secondary factors in your FICO score is the average age of the accounts on your credit reports. The older the average, the better it is for your scores. There's a myth that closing a credit card account will somehow remove that card from consideration in the average age calculation. Here's the real deal: FICO scoring considers open and closed cards when determining the average age of your accounts. Closing the card doesn't remove it from your credit reports, so it's still going to be considered.

Bottom line: Be careful when deciding to close credit card accounts. Reread Myth #2 above for the reason.

Myth #4: Spreading Balances Across Multiple Cards Helps Your Scores.

This is incorrect. First off, there's no hiding credit card debt by doing this. Ten thousand dollars on one card is still the same amount as $1,000 on ten cards. The aggregate revolving utilization percentage (see Myth #2 above) is the same either way, so you gain nothing there. But what you have just done is to increase the number of accounts you have with a balance greater than $0, which is going to lower your scores.

Bottom line: Stop trying to beat the system. Do you think the folks at FICO are idiots? Pay off your credit card debt—stop trying to shuffle it around.

CHAPTER 10

Improving Your FICO Scores by Understanding the Scoring Model

What are credit inquiries and do they hurt my credit scores? And what's this rumor I keep hearing about how FICO scores are protected from multiple inquiries in a short period of time?

ALMOST EVERYTHING YOU'VE EVER WANTED TO KNOW ABOUT CREDIT INQUIRIES

First things first, let's define "credit inquiry." A credit inquiry is simply a record of someone gaining access to your credit reports. The inquiry record has two meaningful components: the date of the access and the name of the party doing the accessing. The credit reporting agencies maintain a record of inquiries from anywhere between six months and twenty-four months, depending on the inquiry type.

All inquiries fall neatly into two categories, hard and soft. Hard inquiries are usually generated when you apply for something (there are exceptions, though). Soft inquiries are generated when access to your credit report is granted for a reason other than the underwriting of an application. Below are just a few examples of each type.

Hard Inquiries	Soft Inquiries
• Mortgage applications • Auto loan applications • Credit card applications • Personal loan applications • Collection agency skip-tracing	• Consumers pulling their own credit files • Lenders sending you a pre-approved credit offer in the mail • Lenders with whom you have an existing relationship viewing your credit periodically

Hard inquiries are what we in the credit-scoring world refer to as "fair game," meaning they are viewed and considered by credit scoring models, lenders, and anyone else who has access to your credit reports. These are the types of inquiries that **can** lower your scores. Notice the obnoxious bolding of the word "can." Hard inquiries don't always lower your scores but they certainly can.

Soft inquiries are off limits. They're off limits to credit scoring models and off limits to lenders. In fact, they aren't shown to anyone other than you when you ask for a copy of your own credit reports. Most credit reports are polluted with soft inquiries, so thankfully they have no impact to your scores, at all.

Just like everything else on your credit reports, there is no fixed value per inquiry. So, when you read things like "My score went down twelve points because of an inquiry" or "Inquiries are worth six points each," you can ignore what you've read because it's incorrect. The number of points you earn in the "inquiry" category is based on how many hard ones you have on your file over the previous twelve months. That's right, hard inquiries over twelve months old don't have any impact on your FICO scores, despite the fact that they'll be on your files for another twelve months.

Now, let's address the method which FICO uses to count inquiries. This is complicated, which is why there's so much incorrect information on the subject floating around the web.

Remember, we're just talking about hard inquiries at this point and only those that have occurred in the previous twelve months.

Thirty-Day "Safe Harbor" Period

Mortgage, auto, and student loan–related inquiries that are less than thirty days old have no impact at all on your FICO scores. That's why the date of the inquiry and the party accessing your reports is so important, because that's how the inquiry is dated and categorized. So, if you want to split hairs, these types of inquiries only count for a maximum of eleven months, because they're ignored for their first thirty days on file and then only counted until they're up to one year old.

Forty-Five-Day "Rate Shopping Allowance"

Over a decade ago, FICO changed how they treat multiple inquiries caused by lenders in the mortgage and auto lending industries. And more recently, they've changed how they treat student loan inquiries. The issue was how to not penalize consumers who were interest-rate shopping, and thus filling their credit reports with multiple inquiries in a very short period of time. The forty-five-day logic considers inquiries from mortgage, auto, and student loan lenders that occur within forty-five days of each other as one inquiry. So, you can apply for fifteen auto loans and as long as the lenders pull your reports within a forty-five-day period, the fifteen inquiries will be counted by the FICO score as only one search for credit. The idea, which makes perfect sense, is that the shopper is really only looking for one loan, not fifteen. There was a time when the forty-five-day period was only fourteen days, but that was in much older versions of the scoring software.

You've probably noticed that credit cards, retail store cards, and gasoline cards are not protected. That's because people don't generally shop for plastic like they'd shop for an auto loan. You don't apply for credit cards with Capital One, Discover, American Express, Bank of America, and Wells Fargo, and then choose whichever issuer gave you the best deal. What you've actually done is to open new cards with Capital One, Discover, American Express, Bank of America, and Wells Fargo, and opening so many accounts in such a small period of time is indicative of elevated credit risk.

The same is true for retail store cards. You don't rate shop at Macy's stores at every mall in your city. The rate you get is going to be the same regardless of which store you apply at. This is very troubling news for the people who use their credit reports as "15 percent off" coupons at the mall and apply for instant credit at the register just to save a few bucks. Each of those is really an application for a new store credit card, and those inquiries can sting.

There are also some notable exceptions to the rule that the hard inquiry is always seen and considered. For example, employment inquiries do not count in your credit scores. Neither do insurance or utility inquiries. As you can imagine, it's hard to argue that applying for a job, insurance (which is generally a legal or lender requirement), or utilities leads to a debt obligation and you certainly don't want to penalize people for applying for these basic needs.

There you have it. Everything you ever wanted to know about inquiries, but were too afraid to ask.

UNDERSTANDING CREDIT CARD UTILIZATION

Credit card utilization is one of most important factors in your credit scores. And, if done properly, lowering your utilization percentage is the most actionable way to improve your scores. Credit card utilization, also called revolving utilization, is complicated and often misunderstood and misreported. You'll need your credit reports and a calculator as I'll walk you through this.

What the heck is credit card utilization? Credit card utilization is the relationship between the balances on your credit card accounts and the credit limits on all of those accounts.

It is expressed as a percentage and is calculated in a number of ways. It's so important that it is a key factor in the "debt" category of your FICO credit score. The debt category is worth 30 percent of your FICO score points, and while the credit card utilization percentage alone isn't worth all 30 percent (myth), it's certainly key to earning and maintaining great scores.

Line Item Utilization: Calculate This First

The first way to calculate your credit card utilization is by doing so for each one of your cards. So, go grab each and every one of your credit cards, retail store cards, and gasoline cards and make a stack. As long as they have revolving terms, meaning you don't have to pay them in full each month, they need to be in your pile.

Each of those cards has a credit limit, which is the highest amount that can be charged on that card. You can find the limit by looking at a statement or by calling the credit card issuer. Or you can look at your credit report. Getting the limits from your credit reports is the most useful method (because that's how credit scores calculate utilization), but they aren't 100 percent accurate 100 percent of the time.

For every card that has a balance (meaning you got a bill this month), divide that balance by the credit limit. Then multiply that figure by 100 and you'll get the utilization percentage on that card. So, if you have a $50 balance and a $500 credit limit, you'll get 10 percent. Your goal is to have the lowest possible percentages.

Now, you're going to be tempted to cheat. Just because you already did—or plan to—pay the balance in full, doesn't mean your percentage is zero. Credit scores can't tell what your intentions are, and as long as the balance is showing up on your credit report, then you will have a utilization percentage greater than zero.

NOTE: Sometimes credit limits don't show up on credit reports. This is what I was referring to earlier about those limits not being accurate 100 percent of the time. If your report has missing credit limits on open credit card accounts, then you're not out of the woods. Look for the field called "High Balance" and use that figure in lieu of the missing credit limit. The high balance is the historical highest balance on that account.

Aggregate Utilization: Calculate This Second

The method for calculating aggregate utilization is exactly the same as it was for line item utilization except for one difference. You'll need to add together all of the balances on your credit cards and all of the credit limits as well. Then you'll divide the aggregate balance by the aggregate limit.

Now, it's important you do this right. Just because you have a credit card that doesn't have a balance, doesn't mean it won't count here. You'll still include the credit limit, which will help your percentage. This is the number one reason you don't want to close credit card accounts even if you don't use (or want) the card any longer. The unused limit helps your utilization percentage.

What's a Good Percentage?

According to FICO, the consumers who have the highest scores in the country (760 and above) have an aggregate utilization of 7 percent. That's about as clean of an answer as you're ever going to get to a FICO score question. Of course, that doesn't prevent people from giving answers that are all over the place. I've seen 30 percent, and I've seen 50 percent, and I've even seen 70 percent.

The way the scores are designed rewards consumers for having a lower rather than higher utilization. So generally, the lower the number, the more points you're going to earn in your score. Thirty is better than 50, but not as good as 7. And I'm not sure where in the world someone got 70 percent. That's just terrible.

IF YOU WANT TO IMPROVE YOUR FICO SCORES, PAYING OFF CREDIT DEBT REIGNS SUPREME

When it comes to boosting your FICO credit scores, there are a variety of strategies that will yield varying amounts of improvement. Many people believe that getting negative information removed from your credit reports is the number one way to increase your scores. This is true, but only if the consumer is successful at getting most, if not all, of the negative information removed. Getting one of your twelve collections removed isn't going to do anything for your scores.

A much more actionable (and realistic) way to increase your scores is to pay off debt. Not only is this a proven way to earn better scores, but it's also practically immediate. Paying down debt can result in a better score in less than thirty days, which is lightning fast in the slow-moving credit reporting environment.

But before you crack open your checkbook, you'll want to consider *which* debt you're going to eliminate. Why? Because when it comes to improving your credit scores, not all "debt elimination" is created equal. In fact, paying some huge debts will yield little to no score improvement, while paying smaller debts can result in a meaningful score boost.

Using a scoring tool built by FICO (available at myFICO .com), I recently simulated the following "pay off" scenarios and measured their impact to a FICO score of 630, which is clearly one that you'd like to improve. In each scenario, the factors below were the only things changed on the credit report:

A. Paying off a $250,000 mortgage loan
B. Paying off a $35,000 auto loan
C. Paying off a $5,000 credit card balance
D. Paying off a $1,000 collection balance

The results:

A. **Paying off a mortgage loan of $250,000 improved FICO 630 to FICO 635**

I've been telling people for many years that installment debt, even in large amounts, doesn't have much of an impact to your scores. This is the quantification of that advice. And while this is just a simulation, in 2010 I sold a house and eliminated a $249,000 mortgage and my FICO scores went up four points.

B. **Paying off an auto loan of $35,000 improved FICO 630 to FICO 635**

An auto loan is an installment loan (like a mortgage), and the effect of paying it off is equally unimpressive from a scoring perspective. Don't get me wrong; it's nice not having a monthly car payment. And it'll save you big bucks not paying interest on a $35,000 loan any longer.

C. **Paying off a credit card balance of $5,000 improved FICO 630 to FICO 665**

Eliminating the credit card debt resulted in the largest improvement to the credit score, and really, it wasn't even a close race. Credit card debt is scientifically proven to be a riskier type of credit for lenders to extend, which means even smaller amounts like what was used in the simulation can have a significant impact to your FICO scores. It also means if you can pay it off, your scores will improve a lot, and very quickly. And even if you can't pay off your credit cards 100 percent, your scores will still improve by paying it down as much as possible.

D. **Paying off a collection balance of $1,000 dropped FICO 630 to FICO 595**

Unfortunately, this is an all-too-common occurrence, as any of you with collections have probably experienced. There's a deficiency in the credit reporting system that shows recent activity on an otherwise older collection account on your credit reports if you make a payment. This recent activity makes the collection look younger and can result in a score drop. In my simulation, the recentness of the collection went from "greater than three years old" to "less than twelve months." When you make a payment on a collection, the collection agency will report the new balance to the credit reporting agencies. The "date reported" on the collection account will then be the current date, which can lead to the score drop.

These results, while simulated, are a very accurate reflection of what will likely happen to your scores if you pay off one of these items. So, if you want to pay off a car loan or a mortgage loan early, do so because it'll save you money in interest. Don't think that your scores are going to shoot through the roof.

CHAPTER 11

Delinquencies & the Seven Deadly FICO Sins

There are but a few certainties in life: death, taxes, and FICO not disclosing how many "points" certain events can cost your FICO scores. But in March 2011, the scoring giant did just that: provided some clarity on how many points you can lose by doing a variety of "bad" things.

IMPACT OF MORTGAGE DELINQUENCIES ON YOUR FICO SCORES

Here's what we already knew: delinquencies are bad, severe delinquencies are usually worse, and recent and frequent delinquencies are the worst.

As a result of FICO's study results, we also now know:

For Someone with a FICO Score of 680
- A thirty-day delinquency and a ninety-day delinquency have the SAME score impact. Both of these events

will turn a 680 into a score somewhere between 600 and 620.

- A short sale (settlement) with a deficiency balance (the remaining balance owed to the lender after they have disposed of the property) will have the same score impact as a foreclosure. The events will turn a 680 into a score somewhere between 575 and 595.

- A bankruptcy is the worst thing that can happen to your FICO scores. It will turn a 680 into a score somewhere between 530 and 550.

- The amount of time for your score to recover back to a 680 is nine months for a thirty-day or ninety-day delinquency, but it takes much longer to recover from anything worse. Short sales, settlements, and foreclosures all take three years to recover fully. A bankruptcy will take you five years to recover.

Impact to FICO Score

	Consumer A	Consumer B	Consumer C
Starting FICO score	~680	~720	~780
FICO score after these events:			
Thirty days late on mortgage	600–620	630–650	670–690
Ninety days late on mortgage	600–620	610–630	650–670
Short sale/deed-in-lieu/ settlement (no deficiency balance)	610–630	605–635	655–675
Short sale (with deficiency balance)	575–595	570–590	620–640
Foreclosure	575–595	570–590	620–640
Bankruptcy	530–550	525–545	540–560

Source: FICO's *Banking Analytics Blog*

For Someone with a FICO Score of 780

- A thirty-day delinquency and a ninety-day delinquency have a different score impact. The thirty-day late turns the 780 into a score somewhere between 670 and 690. A ninety-day delinquency will turn the 780 into a 650–670.

- A short sale (settlement), with a deficiency balance, will again have the same score impact as a foreclosure. The events will turn a 780 into a score somewhere between 620 and 640.

- The amount of time for your score to recover back to a 780 is much longer than the amount of time for your 680 to recover. It takes three years to recover from a thirty-day delinquency and seven years to recover from a ninety-day delinquency, a short sale, or a foreclosure. It will take you seven to ten years to recover from a bankruptcy.

Estimated Time for FICO Score to Recover Fully

	Consumer A	Consumer B	Consumer C
Starting FICO score	~680	~720	~780
FICO score after these events:			
30 days late on mortgage	~9 months	~2.5 years	~3 years
90 days late on mortgage	~9 months	~3 years	~7 years
Short sale/deed-in-lieu/ settlement (no deficiency balance)	~3 years	~7 years	~7 years
Short sale (with deficiency balance)	~3 years	~7 years	~7 years
Foreclosure	~3 years	~7 years	~7 years
Bankruptcy	~5 years	~7–10 years	~7–10 years

Note: Estimates assume all else held constant over time (e.g., no new account openings, no new delinquency, similar outstanding debt).
Source: FICO's *Banking Analytics Blog*

What I found to be especially important is the fact that a payment that's even just one cycle past due (thirty-day delinquency) has a profound negative impact on your scores. This is problematic, especially for consumers who have chosen to be delinquent on their mortgages in an attempt to get help under the Making Home Affordable plans. "Consumers may be told in some cases that they have to go late before they can get any help under one of the HAMP [Home Affordable Modification Program] programs," says Joanne Gaskin, director of FICO's Global Scoring Unit. "It's important for them [consumers] to understand that even a thirty-day late can be very damaging."

This study also seems to finally put to bed the ongoing myth that short sales are better for your credit scores than foreclosures. "There seems to be a perceived view that a short sale is going to be significantly different to your FICO score than a foreclosure," according to Gaskin. "While there's a minor difference, it's not significant."

THE SEVEN DEADLY FICO SCORE SINS
TO AVOID AT ALL COSTS

When was the last time you applied for an auto loan, a mortgage, or a personal loan? Do you remember signing paperwork or agreeing to certain terms online by clicking the infamous "click here if you agree" box? Well, that piece of paper that you signed, and didn't really read and probably don't understand, is called a promissory note. It's essentially your memorialized promise to pay someone else some sum of money under certain terms.

Those "certain terms" are not negotiable and they're not suggestions. They are actual terms that lenders must demand be followed. Not following those terms is a huge problem for debtors (you) because they can lead to a default. And, of course, a default isn't exactly what you want showing up on your credit reports, because it will stick around for a whopping seven years and can cause your scores to plummet.

Nobody has ever accused the world of consumer credit of being devoid of humor, and the reporting of defaults is no exception. They can be reported a variety of ways to your credit files, and each variation has a specific meaning. But what is consistent is the fact that they're all considered negative by FICO scoring and other credit scoring systems.

What Does a Default Look Like on a Credit Report? Let Me Count the Ways

1. Settlements   You've defaulted on your promissory note, and now the lender is willing to accept less than you owe them and consider the loan to be settled, but not paid in full. This is very common in the credit card industry, especially in the past few years.

2. Charge-Offs   A charge-off is an accounting designation to identify debt that the lender has determined to be uncollectable. They've written off the debt and now want to realize the tax benefit of doing so.

3. Voluntary Repossessions   This is when you decide to take your car back to the dealership or bank, hand in the keys, and call it a day. Some people think this is a more dignified way to be done with your auto loan or lease. It might seem that way, but you've defaulted on your agreement to make payments. The only thing you've done is avoid the embarrassment (and cost) of having a visit from the repo man.

4. Involuntary Repossessions   This is the exact same thing as a voluntary repo except you decided that you'd rather have the bank hire someone to come get it with the hopes that you'll end up on Operation Repo.

5. Foreclosure   This is a much more common occurrence in the past three years. This is the process whereby the mortgage lender takes physical possession of your home because it's in default. There are a variety of ways to default on a mortgage loan, but for the purposes of this discussion, let's just say the homeowner stopped making his or her payments. There are a lot of moving parts to a foreclosure and this certainly isn't meant to cover them all, but it can lead to an embarrassing visit from the local sheriff, who knocks on your door at 8 a.m. and stands there while you empty your possessions onto the front lawn.

6. *Forfeiture of Deed*   As the rubber meets the road, this is the same as a foreclosure, except you've chosen to leave rather than force the lender to have you evicted. This is also called "forfeiture of deed in lieu of foreclosure," which is exactly how it would show up on your credit reports. Despite the fact that you cooperated and communicated with the mortgage lender, you've still defaulted on your loan obligation.

7. *Short Sales*   This one gets me worked up like you have no idea. A short sale is when the lender agrees to take less than you owe on the home and consider the loan to be paid. This is actually a very good way to dispose of a bad mortgage, because the value of the home is generally higher than it would be if it was taken back and resold out of foreclosure. That's also better for the local neighborhood, because it takes a smaller bite out of the home values. The problem with short sales is that they've only just recently become a common option. And, as with anything new, there is immense confusion and flat-out misrepresentation about the process and the impact it will have on your credit. So, I won't mince words: a short sale is just as bad for your credit as a foreclosure or any of the other aforementioned defaults. They are reported as either charge-offs or settlements, both of which are accurate. There are small armies of real estate agents who are trying to drum up business by pretending short sales are actually better for your credit scores.

So there you have it: the seven deadly FICO sins. These all represent some form of default on a credit obligation. And while this is certainly not an exhaustive list of items that can damage your FICO scores, it's a very good list to avoid.

CHAPTER 12

A Perfect Score

You are more likely to land on the moon than to achieve a FICO score of 850. Who is actually scoring FICO 850? Is that even possible?

CAN I SCORE THAT ELUSIVE FICO 850?

The published score range of the FICO score is 300 to 850. Having said that, the range really isn't 300 to 850, except (per FICO) in their newest scoring system, called FICO 8. The range is actually somewhere *between* 300 and 850. The actual range of the score depends on the variety and generation of FICO scores being used to score your credit reports.

Many of you who have closed on mortgages over the past few years probably recall that you received a "credit score disclosure" document from your mortgage lender (a legal requirement since 2004). That document not only shows your scores, but also in some cases shows the possible range of those scores. You may have noticed that it's not always 300 to 850.

The maximum score held by a US consumer is 844. There is a consumer in Illinois who has achieved that score. There are also consumers who live in New York, Florida, New Jersey, and Pennsylvania who have FICO scores of 834. Pretty much every other state tops out at 831.

Keep a few things in mind. This is the generic FICO score and not the semi-customized version used by some credit card issuers and auto lenders. And this is *not* any score you are given for free online. Some of the freebies top out at well over 900 and give the impression that you've got an impressive FICO score.

And while I've never seen a verified example of someone with FICO 850, as consumers we are certainly getting closer to perfection than we are to utter disaster. We're much closer to the top end of the published range than we are to the bottom end of 300. In fact, all but a few of the worst-performing consumers are well over 100 points away from that imperfect FICO score.

The lowest score held by a US consumer is 387. That honor goes to a consumer living in the state of Virginia. That 387 is by far the lowest of the low. The second lowest is 404 (out of New York). There are also some 407s in Ohio and Texas.

The lowest maximum score is 818, which belongs to a consumer living in Arkansas, and the highest minimum score is 462, which belongs to a consumer living in Vermont.

The lowest average score is 657 and that honor goes to Mississippi. The highest average score is 717, from the state of Wisconsin. My home state of Georgia has nothing to brag about. We're tied for fourth lowest with an average score of 667. In fact, seven of the lowest scoring ten states are in the South.

So it seems like FICO 850 remains out of our reach, which frankly isn't a big deal. You certainly don't need FICO 850 to get what you want with a great rate. As long as you have 760s across the board at all three of the credit reporting agencies, you're in great shape and can end your search for the elusive 850.

SHOOTING FOR FICO 850? HERE'S WHY YOU SHOULDN'T

It's been drilled into our heads recently that "lender's standards are going higher while our FICO scores are headed lower." This divergence in underwriting standards and scores is bad news for a whole lot of people: the roughly 70 million who now score below 650. And those of you who are smart have made some effort to increase your scores so you can enjoy the most "shopper friendly" credit environment in twenty years.

If you've already found yourself in the land of the 780s, it's time to take your foot off the accelerator because you're good—really good. Any further efforts have you officially beating a dead horse and attempts to take the magic number any higher could land you back in the land of the 720s.

Here's what you need to hear . . .

There Is No Incremental Value to Being Higher Than 780

Other than bragging rights, there's really no reason to stress out about your scores if they're already over 780. Even in today's credit environment, a 780 puts you about twenty points to the good and you've now found yourself squarely among the credit elite. You will likely get whatever you're applying for at the best rates and terms the lender or insurance company has to offer.

As of September 2010, a 780 FICO score gets you a credit card at 7.9 percent (issued by a credit union). It also gets you auto financing from a captive lender (the manufacturer's finance arm) for as low as 0 percent on selected models. And even if captive financing isn't an option for you, a 780 gets you rates as low as 5.2 percent for a new car. And if you're trying to buy a home, a 780 (along with satisfying other non-credit criteria) gets you a rate around 4 percent, which is crazy low.

The point is, your rates, premiums, and terms will be no better at FICO 810, 830, or 850 than they are at 780.

You Can Do More Harm Than Good

If I've said it once, I've said it a thousand times . . . credit scores move like water. They're going to take the path of least resistance. That means a score of 780 is easier to turn into a 680 than it is to turn it into an 800.

This is especially true for people with young (age) or thin (number of accounts) credit files. The good people at Mint.com have told me that many of their *MintLife* readers are in their twenties. And if you look at the comments to my student loan debt story, I kind of get that same idea.

Something that you won't see from reading online stories about credit scoring models is that fact that young people generally have younger credit reports (duh). That's determined by calculating the average age of the accounts on your credit reports by looking at the "date opened" of your accounts. And the younger the credit file, the more volatile the score. In English, this means your scores are going to react to changes in your credit data more significantly than someone who has had credit for decades.

If you apply for and open a new account, apply for a credit line increase, max out a credit card, miss a payment, have a collection show up on your credit report, or experience a variety of other credit incidents, your scores are likely to be damaged disproportionately to someone who has a well-aged credit report. This is because you don't have as much positive compensatory information to offset the bad stuff.

Yes, Your Scores Can Actually Be Too High

Some lenders don't want an abundance of customers whose scores are too high. Stratospheric scores, those well into the 800s, generally belong to people who don't use credit. And those who don't use credit don't generate income.

For the first time ever, there's now a sweet spot, credit score–wise. You really want to fall between 760 and 810, give or take a few points in either direction. The 760 means you're a very good credit risk. It also means you're probably using credit, have credit card balances, and have installment loans. This means you're generating revenue for your lenders and credit card issuers.

If you score too high, it means you are probably not using credit cards. You're a very good credit risk, but that's not good enough in today's credit environment. The lender wants and needs to make some dough, and if your score indicates that you're a great credit risk, but have poor revenue potential, then they might just decline you. Yes, you can get declined for having too high of a score. It's called a "high side override," meaning you scored higher than the lender's low-end criteria, but they still declined you.

So for those of you who are at 760–780, your journey has ended. Sit back and enjoy the view from atop the FICO score mountain!

For the Haters

Save it. This isn't score obsession. As long as lenders, insurance companies, utility companies, and landlords use credit scoring to determine rates, premiums, deposit requirements, and terms (and employers use credit reports as part of employment screening), it's something we have to take seriously.

You can't "choose" not to be under the influence of your credit reports and credit scores. That's not possible. Having good credit reports and scores, and paying less for things (your mortgage, your car loan, and your insurance) is a "Top Five" wealth-building tool. Trying to earn a great FICO score is no different than checking the performance and allocation of your investments. The minute credit reports and credit scores cease to have importance, I promise I'll start working on a book about knitting.

CHAPTER 13

Access to Free Credit Scores

A much anticipated change to the Fair Credit Reporting Act (FCRA) went live on January 1, 2011, and gave consumers a peek inside the practice of what's referred to as risk-based pricing. Risk-based pricing is the practice whereby lenders assign the terms and conditions on credit cards and other credit-related products commensurate with the applicant's level of credit risk.

AN INSIDE LOOK AT RISK-BASED PRICING

The better your credit, the better your deal. If you have great credit, you'll get terms that not everyone will get. If you have poor credit, you might get approved, but not at the best terms. This is the standard operating procedure in almost all credit environments including mortgage, credit card, and auto lending. The lenders "base" their "pricing" on your "risk," hence the term: risk-based pricing.

The new risk-based pricing rules now require that a lender who approves an application, but not at their best rate, give the applicant one of two disclosures. The disclosure options are as follows:

The Risk-Based Pricing Notice

This option will inform the new customer that he or she did not get the best deal (interest rate or credit limit for example) from the lender and that their decision was made, in part, based on data from a credit report. The customer now has two months to claim a free credit report from the credit reporting agency that provided the lender with the credit information.

The Credit Score Disclosure Notice

This option will provide the new customer with a variety of things having to do with the score used by the lender to make their decision. First, the actual score used by the lender will be shared with the new customer. This marks the first time consumers will be given their actual scores from lenders, outside of the mortgage environment, which has had a credit score disclosure requirement since the 2003 amendment to the Fair Credit Reporting Act.

In most cases, the score disclosed will be your FICO credit score, which is designed and developed by FICO. In addition to your actual FICO score, you'll also be provided with the numeric range of the score, which is published as 300 to 850. You'll also be told where you rank, score-wise, compared to the overall US population. And, as with the risk-based pricing notice, you'll be told how to claim your free credit report.

NOTE: In both of the above notice options, the letters will direct you where to get your credit report. In the risk-based pricing notice, the report will come directly from the credit bureau that provided the data to the lender and it will *not* count against your annual free credit report allocation. In the credit score disclosure notice, the report will come from www.AnnualCreditReport.com and it *will* count against your annual free credit report allocation.

What the New Rules Do Not Mandate

The risk-based pricing rules only apply to adverse approvals (approvals where you didn't get the best deal), and they only apply to financial services companies. They do not apply if you've been flat-out denied credit, and they do not apply to insurance companies, utility companies, and property management companies . . . all of whom use credit reports and scores to make decisions about your terms.

Additionally, the choice of disclosures will be made by the lender and they won't all choose the credit score option. In fact, according to recent reports, Bank of America, Discover, American Express, and SunTrust have chosen the non-score option. Wells Fargo and Capital One have said they will use the score option for credit card customers.

FREE CREDIT SCORES (SERIOUSLY, THEY'RE REALLY FREE)

In the world of credit reporting and credit scoring, the word "free" gets thrown around too liberally, especially when it comes to products and services marketed to consumers via retail websites. "Free" in many cases actually means "conditionally free," which really means it ain't free. This section covers the very limited number of websites where you can actually get a free credit score, with no strings attached.

My criteria here were simple. The score had to be 100 percent free with no credit card information exchanged, meaning there couldn't be any condition under which the consumer would or could get charged. The score also had to be potentially relevant, meaning there had to be a chance that a lender would use the score to make lending-related decisions. Therefore, the score had to be commercially available to lenders.

I couldn't go so far as to say the score had to be the same score used by most lenders, because that would have limited the score option primarily to a FICO score, which isn't available for free anywhere. I left off the many websites that (1) give away scores that aren't available to lenders, (2) give you an approximation (or range) of what your score could be, (3) require you to answer a series of questions in order to simulate your score, and (4) take a credit card number in exchange for a free score and begin charging you if you don't cancel a trial credit-monitoring subscription.

My criteria left two websites standing, CreditSesame.com and CreditKarma.com.

CreditSesame.com

- *What You Get*: CreditSesame provides a free credit score and a summarized version of the data on your Experian credit report. This free access to your credit report doesn't count against your free annual credit report allotment. That's a nice bonus on top of the free score. The credit report data is displayed differently than what you'd see if you pulled your credit report directly from Experian, but it's still easy to read and understand.

    The score you get is your Experian National Equivalency Score. "We selected it because we feel it best approximates the range of the FICO score that is most familiar to consumers," says Tony Wahl, lending information manager at CreditSesame. "The National Equivalency Score is commercially available to lenders," according to Kristine Snyder, public relations manager at Experian. "The score range is 360 to 840."

- *How Often You Can Get It*: "The score comes automatically once a month. You don't have to request it over and over again," according to Wahl. This autopilot approach is nice because you don't have to remember to request an updated score, which makes it much more valuable than if it were a "one and done" freebie. And the fact that it comes monthly gives your Experian credit report enough time to go through an entire set of monthly updates from your lenders. That means your newer scores will reflect a fully updated Experian credit report, thus giving you a good idea as to your score movement vis-à-vis your monthly credit activity.

- *Credit Card Required*: Nope
- *Trial Membership Required*: Nope
- *Here's the Catch*: Neither of the companies that I've included here are nonprofit, which means they are in business to make money. So how does CreditSesame make money? CreditSesame makes money by advertising loan products such as first mortgages, second mortgages, and auto loans. Their model is somewhat unique, as they only get a bounty if the consumer actually gets a loan, rather than just applying for a loan or clicking through to a lender's website. "We only make money when a consumer closes their loan with one of our lending partners. We win only if the consumer wins," says Wahl.

CreditKarma.com

- *What You Get*: CreditKarma provides two different credit risk scores for free. You can get your TransRisk score, and you can also get your VantageScore. Both scores are based on the data in your TransUnion credit file. And both TransRisk and VantageScore are commercially available to lenders. In fact, VantageScore is largely viewed as FICO's most potentially significant competitor, as it's marketed and distributed by all three of the national credit reporting agencies.

Like CreditSesame, CreditKarma also provides a summarized version of your credit report via their Credit Report Card. The tool slices apart your TransUnion credit report and summarizes key categories much like a credit scoring system would. I like this method of display and apparently I'm not the only one. "One of our most popular tools, in addition to the free scores, is the Credit Report Card," says Kenneth Lin, CEO of CreditKarma.

- *How Often You Can Get It*: "We actually allow you to update your scores every day, in real time," according to Lin. We both had a good laugh when I asked him "what were you thinking?" with the decision to allow consumers to get their updated scores every day.
- *Credit Card Required*: Nope
- *Trial Membership Required*: Nope
- *Here's the Catch*: CreditKarma is a lead aggregator, or lead generation website. They attempt to guide traffic to a variety of lender partners where you can apply for financial service products, primarily credit cards and mortgages. According to Lin, "We sell advertising that displays credit card offers and mortgage offers. CreditKarma also gets a revenue share if you were to apply for a credit card offer displayed on our site." This is not an uncommon business model and is shared by many other companies.

FELL FOR A "FREE" CREDIT REPORT? YOU MAY BE PART OF A CLASS ACTION SUIT

Have you ever heard of a company called ConsumerInfo.com? You probably have not, but chances are you've heard of (or seen) FreeCreditReport.com and FreeCreditScore.com. Both of those sites are owned by ConsumerInfo.com and guess who owns ConsumerInfo.com . . . Experian.

On March 22, 2011, David Waring, a consumer who lives in San Diego, filed a class action lawsuit against ConsumerInfo.com, essentially Experian, because of the actions of FreeCreditReport.com and FreeCreditScore.com. As with all class action lawsuits, there is a large number of potential class members. Could *you* be a member of the class? Read on to find out.

The plaintiff alleges that he and other consumers who signed up for services via the aforementioned sites were deceived because the credit score provided by ConsumerInfo.com is not the actual score sold to lenders, yet their advertising suggests that it is used by lenders to assess creditworthiness. The score on their websites is the PLUS Score, which isn't even commercially available to lenders, so it can't be used to determine your creditworthiness. Experian discloses as much: "Calculated on the PLUS Score model, your Experian Credit Score indicates your relative credit risk level for educational purposes and is not the score used by lenders."

The problem is that on another one of their sites they state that "Your Free Credit Score Matters" and "Your credit scores determine the amount credit lenders will make available to you and the interest rates and payments on mortgages, credit cards, auto loans, insurance policies, and more." This, of course, isn't true because none of the aforementioned lenders use your "Free Credit Score" for anything. Further, there is no disclosure in their ubiquitous television ads about how the score you get for free is not used by lenders.

The core service offered by the ConsumerInfo sites (and there are a lot more than just the two mentioned in the lawsuit) is actually a credit monitoring service that includes a free score as the "loss leader" to get consumers to sign up. Despite the use of the word "free" in the URL, the services aren't actually free. There is a trial period of seven days and if you don't cancel your trial credit monitoring service during that time frame, your credit card, which you gave them when you signed up, is charged $14.95 each month until you do cancel. At best I'd call this "conditionally free."

Experian has gotten their hands slapped by the Federal Trade Commission in the past for how they market their "free credit report" services. They've paid two fines to the FTC equaling $1.25 million because of deceptive sales practices. The Credit Card Accountability, Responsibility, and Disclosure Act (CARD Act) of 2009 even addresses how free credit reports can be marketed, which is funny considering the CARD Act was meant to curb egregious practices of credit card issuers (see Chapter 24 for more about the CARD Act).

The CARD Act states that websites that give away free credit reports must contain the following mandatory disclosure across the top of each and every webpage that mentions free credit reports:

> THIS NOTICE IS REQUIRED BY LAW. Read more at FTC.GOV. You have the right to a free credit report at AnnualCreditReport.com or at 877-322-8228, the ONLY authorized source under federal law.

Experian, in response, simply started charging $1 for their "free" credit report and then subsequently changed their marketing focus to free credit scores instead of free credit reports. If you haven't figured it out already, the marketing of free credit *scores* does not require the above mandatory disclosure. As I said in an interview with the *New York Times*, Experian remains two steps ahead of the FTC.

I reached out to Experian regarding the litigation and this was their statement: "Experian's practice is not to comment on pending or ongoing litigation involving the company."

The lawsuit class "period" covers the time frame from March 22, 2007, to March 2011, although this can change. This means everyone who purchased services from FreeCreditReport.com, FreeCreditScore.com, or ConsumerInfo.com during that four-year period could be a member of the class. Clearly, this means the class size could number in the millions.

I've been involved in several class action lawsuits as an expert witness, and these types of cases can take years to resolve. As such, we should not expect news any time soon, and we certainly should not expect a quick resolution.

PART III

Credit Cards

CHAPTER 14

Credit Card Offers: Behind the Scenes

It's a very simple question with a very complicated answer. Exactly how does a credit card solicitation find its way into your mailbox? And once we've covered that, we'll discuss something that is probably even more important to many of you: how can you stop the offers?

HOW DOES A CREDIT CARD OFFER END UP IN YOUR MAILBOX?

I don't think most people understand just how many moving parts there are "behind the scenes," all with the goal of getting a card into your back pocket or purse. The chronology of events that occur prior to an offer being made is long and fairly misunderstood.

Step 1: The Decision

Credit card issuers don't do anything arbitrarily, especially when deciding whether or not to market a credit card to an individual or a group of individuals. The decision is generally one that's based on a variety of metrics, including, but not limited to, take rate (the percentage of consumers who will actually bite on a credit card offer, a.k.a. "response rate"), activation rate (the percentage of approved applicants who will activate the card when received), usage rate (the percentage of approved and activated card holders who will actually use it), and profit and loss (the amount of revenue generated by the cardholders minus write-offs and overhead).

If a card issuer determines that marketing a specific type of card to a specific consumer or geographical area will yield a large number of users who will generate enough revenue . . . then we're on to step 2.

Step 2: The Prospecting

Walk to your mailbox almost any day and it'll be filled with credit card offers. Why your mailbox? Again, it's not arbitrary. It's based on hundreds of decision variables, which are often called the "selection criteria."

In order for you to get one of those offers, the credit card issuer has to believe that you meet their criteria for credit risk. That's usually one of the most important traits in the issuer's mind. How in the world do they know what kind of risk you pose if you haven't applied for credit? Here's where it gets fun . . .

The credit reporting agencies all have massive databases and you're in all of them. And unless you've "opted out" of receiving pre-approved credit card offers (see the second half of this chapter), they're selling your information to credit card issuers for their prospecting purposes. Don't get me wrong, they're not actually selling your credit reports, yet. They're just selling the issuers a list of consumers and addresses that meet their criteria for credit risk. Follow me . . .

John's Bank wants to test-market a new credit card in the Atlanta market. Let's say hypothetically my bank wants to acquire 5,000 new test customers in that area. But I don't want just any 5,000 customers. I want 5,000 customers with FICO scores greater than 720.

So, my next step is to tell the credit bureau that I want to buy a list of consumers who all live in Atlanta (I'll give them a zip code list to go from), and all have FICO scores greater than 720. The credit bureaus then take that criteria and provide me with "counts"—the volume of consumers who meet my relatively simple requirements. Let's say 2,500,000 people meet the "Atlanta plus FICO 720" criteria.

I can buy the entire list of 2,500,000 prospects if I want. But remember, I only want to take on 5,000 new customers for my small test. A typical response rate for a credit card solicitation mail campaign is about half of 1 percent, which means if I mail my offer to all 2,500,000 people, I will likely end up with 12,500 new customers. That's too many for my test. What does the bank do?

The next step in the process is for the list to get cut down to a size that will likely yield a number of new customers with which I'm more comfortable. And since the response rate will likely be about half a percent, I tell the credit bureau that I just want 1,000,000 prospects.

Step 3: The Deployment

Now that we've determined that 1,000,000 prospects will leave me with 5,000 new customers, it's time for me to send them the offer. The credit card issuers don't do this in house. They'll outsource the process to a professional mail house that will take delivery of the entire list of 1,000,000 prospects and merge their names and addresses on the credit card offer and drop them in the mail.

At this point, the mail house sends the credit bureau a list of everyone who was sent an offer. It won't be exactly 1,000,000 because some will be dropped because of address and other issues. The credit bureau takes that list and posts promotional inquiries on their credit reports.

Step 4: The Delivery

A few days later you get home from work, check your mail, and find a new credit card offer from John's Bank. Ninety-nine percent of you will trash it straight away. But half of a percent of you will open it and find the offer appealing enough to fill out the accompanying application and send it back to me for processing. What have you just done? You've technically applied for credit with John's Bank.

When I get the application back from you, I'll pull your full credit report and score. I do this to set the final terms of the card, including the rate and the credit limit. Technically, since I used credit report screening, I have to offer you something. That's the law. It's called a "firm offer of credit or insurance."

There are ways around that requirement, though, like if you just filed bankruptcy the day before. But most of you will get a new card with a super cool John's Bank logo on it. Within thirty days an innocuous envelope shows up in your mail with a Delaware return address. You open it and see your new card. And after you call to activate the card, I'm happy to call you a new customer of John's Bank. Welcome!

HOW CAN I STOP THE CREDIT CARD OFFERS?

Now that you understand how these dozens of credit card offers end up in your mailbox every month, you're probably wondering, how can you *stop* them?

As I just described, the credit reporting agencies, in addition to selling credit reports and credit scores, sell lists of consumer names and addresses to credit card issuers so they can send you those offers. The list of consumers has been "screened" by the credit reporting agencies and meets certain minimum credit score requirements. For example, a bank can buy a list of consumers who have FICO scores greater than 650, thus eliminating very risky prospective customers.

Thankfully, there is a way to have your name removed from those screened lists. And, even better news, it's free to do so. By going to the website I'm about to share, you can have your name removed for five years or even permanently. But don't worry; you can always opt back in if your mailbox starts having separation anxiety.

Opting out is easy, but giving out the amount of information you'll be asked to give is going to be hard. You've got to provide your name, address, Social Security Number, state of birth, and phone number. They need this information to ensure the correct credit file has been "blocked" for screening purposes.

Some people don't like the opting-out idea because they can get a proxy of their credit scores by the offers they're receiving. For example, if you're getting platinum-style offers, then you've got great credit scores. If you're getting "classic" card offers with limits of "up to" $1,000, then your scores aren't that great.

Where to Opt Out of Pre-Approved Credit Card Offers

There is only one legitimate website where you can opt out of being on the credit bureaus' pre-approved mailing lists: www.optoutprescreen.com. This website is a joint venture of the four (remember, there are four) credit reporting agencies, and allowing you to "opt out" is required under the Fair Credit Reporting Act.

Opting out is 100 percent free and any company that attempts to sell you a service that includes opting you out as a feature is doing nothing more than going to this site and opting you out by proxy. So, save your hard-earned cash and do it yourself. Incidentally, you can also opt back in at the same site and yes, that's free as well.

Just because you've opted out doesn't mean you're going to stop getting offers. First off, your name is probably already on several pre-screened lists, and you can't get your name off of them after the lists have been delivered to the lender. And opting out just gets your name removed from screened lists sold by the credit bureaus. It doesn't remove your name from other lists that are sold by other companies, such as alumni associations or magazine subscription list owners.

CHAPTER 15

Credit Card Behaviors & Your Credit Scores

Should I open a new card? Should I close an existing card? I just don't know what to do! Yes, I realize this opening salvo is a grammatical mess, but it is a textual representation of what goes through the minds of consumers every day when they're trying to decide how, when, if, and why to use their credit cards. These scenarios have an upside and a downside, and as always, my goal is to make you aware of the benefits and pitfalls so that you can make a more informed decision.

SHOULD I OPEN A NEW CREDIT CARD?

You certainly wouldn't be the first person to struggle with this question. Opening a new card is not a benign event. Your credit report is pulled by the card issuer, which leaves a credit inquiry on one of your credit reports for the next twenty-four months. This inquiry can lower your score.

If the account is approved, it will likely be reported to all three of your credit reports. That can lower scores because when you add a new account to a credit report (especially a young credit report) it can reduce the average age of your accounts. But the credit limit could net out any damage and actually yield a higher score, especially if the limit is significant.

My Answer: If you need a new credit card, then open one. But use it for convenience and pay your balance in full each and every month. Choose a general-use card like a Visa or MasterCard over retail store cards because the terms are almost always much better.

SHOULD I CLOSE AN EXISTING CARD?

In general, as I discussed earlier, closing credit cards is not a good idea because it can result in a lower credit score. When you close a card, you will likely lose the value of the unused credit limit in your scores. If the card has a really high credit limit and you're carrying debt on other cards, then the damage could be significant.

But there are circumstances that trump the credit scores issues. If you're tempted to spend or overspend, then the card might have to go. Using credit cards is an addiction for some people, and the easiest way for them to avoid excessive debt is to avoid plastic altogether.

My Answer: Try to split the difference. Run the card through a shredder, but leave it open, if possible. That way you can't use it, but you don't run the risk of damaging your credit. And if someday you feel more comfortable carrying plastic money, then call the issuer and have them send you a new card.

IF YOU *DO* CHOOSE TO USE CARDS, CHOOSE WISELY

I believe one of my greatest attributes is that I'm a realist. And, as a realist, I know you are going to use plastic to make purchases, and that's perfectly fine as long as you don't let the plastic ruin your life. But before you decide on the type of plastic to use, consider the following pros and cons of each.

Retail Store Cards

These are cards issued in the name of a retail store or retail chain. The setting of the terms of these cards doesn't follow the same process as credit cards. Why do I say that? Retail store cards always have very high interest rates and very low credit limits.

In fact, if you closed your eyes and I explained that your new card had a 24.9 percent interest rate and a $750 credit limit, you'd think I was describing a subprime credit card reserved for someone with terrible credit. You'd be wrong because I'd be describing a retail store card.

Additionally, retail cards can be used in either the store or the chain. Other than that, they have no usability, which means you'll have to have other cards if you want to shop at other places. Ask yourself a simple question . . . where can I use my Macy's card? The answer to the question: Macy's. This acts as an incentive to open several of these "subprime" credit cards.

The low limits also mean even modest purchases can lead to the card being highly leveraged or "utilized." This is bad news for your credit scores. However, making the same purchase on a general-use credit card like a Visa or Discover could be almost meaningless to your credit scores.

That's not the only way retail credit cards can hurt your credit scores. Applying for a retail credit card at the register may be an extremely unsophisticated way of applying for credit, but it is still a credit application, a fact that many consumers don't realize until it's too late. Here's the chronology of events that occurs when you apply at the register: your credit is pulled, an inquiry is posted to your file, a decision about your application is made, and a new account is possibly issued in your name.

Within thirty to forty-five days, that new account will show up on your credit reports.

None of this sounds problematic, but retail store inquiries are the most damaging type and do not enjoy the same FICO exclusion logic described in Chapter 10. This means if the inquiry is going to lower your score, then it will do so for a full twelve months. Notice I used "score" in the singular. Only one of your three credit reports will be pulled, so the inquiry will only show up on one of your three credit reports, and at worst it will impact only one of your FICO scores.

However, when the new account is opened it will likely be reported to all three of the credit reporting agencies. The minute it hits your reports it will affect what's called your "time in file." This is the category of FICO scoring that rewards or penalizes you for the age of your credit file. Adding a new account, or several of them depending on your shopping aggressiveness, will lower the average age of your accounts and can cause your scores to go down.

The only pros I can think of to using these cards is they don't have annual fees and you will get discount offers periodically, judging by the amount of coupons I get in the mail each week.

General-Use Cards

These are Visa, MasterCard, Discover, and some American Express cards. They usually have pretty competitive rates if you've got good credit, and their credit limits can be well in excess of $30,000. They can also be used almost anywhere that accepts plastic. And, with the recent passage of the CARD Act, consumers are enjoying slightly better treatment from credit card issuers than they enjoyed in the past. That's the good news.

The bad news is that it's easy to get into a lot of credit card debt using these cards, and the higher the balance, the more interest you're paying. Tack on the fairly common annual fees charged by these guys and the tradeoff, which is still better than a retail store card, loses some of its luster.

Charge Cards

Do you know what a charge card is? I'll give you a hint . . . it looks like a credit card, it smells like a credit card, but it isn't a credit card. Charge cards are commonly referred to as "pay in full" products because you're required to pay the balance in full each month. The American Express Green card is a good example of a well-known charge card.

The credit limits on these cards are not published, but trust me, you've got one. It's called a shadow limit. Because of the lack of a credit limit, these cards can sometimes lower your credit scores because of how they're considered when measuring the infamous "utilization" percentage, which is more fully explained in Chapter 10. But that doesn't mean these are bad cards.

Because charge cards must be paid in full each month, you'll be less likely to charge a huge balance, and that means you'll be less likely to get into debt. It also means you won't pay interest with these cards. That's good news, but it's also bad news.

Charge card issuers have to make money and since they're not making it off interest, they're more likely to charge you an annual fee. They are also usually reserved for consumers who have strong credit, which means they're not an option for everyone.

So the next time you're shopping around for a card, keep in mind that all of them have their good points and their bad points. And if none of them sound like your cup of tea, well, maybe you should stick to buying things with paper instead of plastic.

THE DANGERS OF PAYING THE MINIMUM ON YOUR CREDIT CARDS

Because of the CARD Act, creditors must print the amount of time it will take to pay off the card's balance (and interest paid) on the credit card statement if you just made the minimum payment required. I've spoken with many consumers and I can tell you that a lot of people think the information is a misprint.

How can it take twenty-two years to pay off a $15,000 credit card debt? Needless to say, this information is very eye opening and extremely useful.

I have used a couple of real examples to show you the impact of paying the minimum on moderate balances of $680 and $1,424. To make things simple, each example assumes that no more is charged to the account during the time frame and the interest rate is 14.5 percent. You will see how fast interest adds up!

Example 1:

The first example is a bill for $680. If you make the minimum payment of $15 a month, it would take six years to pay. The total amount paid would be $991, with $311 of it in interest charges. This is almost 50 percent of the original bill. If you pay more than the minimum, or $23 a month for three years, you would pay $842 and $162 in interest. You save $149 paying it three years earlier. Either way, it is still a very long time to pay a bill totaling $680.

Monthly Payment	Pay Off	Amount Paid	Interest
$15	6 years	$991	$311
$23	3 years	$842	$162

Example 2:

The next example is a bill for $1,424. Paying the minimum of $28 a month would take twelve years to fully pay off the balance. The payments total $2,662, with $1,238 of it being interest. This is 86 percent of the original bill. If you pay more than the minimum, let's say $49 a month, you would pay the bill off in three years, which is nine years earlier. You pay $1,764 and $341 in interest; the savings of $897 is substantial.

Monthly Payment	Pay Off	Amount Paid	Interest
$28	12 years	$2,662	$1,238
$49	3 years	$1,765	$341

In addition, if you don't pay the bill within the date it is due, a late fee of $35 is added to your bill, and your interest rate could also go up as a result. Look at your cardholder agreement, if you haven't thrown it away, and find the "default rate." That's the rate they can charge if you miss a payment.

I don't know about you, but I don't like paying interest; it is throwing money away. I don't get anything tangible in return for this wasted money. I can think of many things to do with $1,238, or even $341, and using it to pay interest isn't one of them.

CHOOSING WHICH CARD TO PAY OFF FIRST

No, this isn't going to be yet another regurgitated advice piece telling you to pay off the cards with the highest interest rates first because you'll save money. Anyone who suggests that's the best and only way to prioritize cards for accelerated payback is simply scratching the surface of the options and is only looking at the problem from one dimension: interest rates. The next time you're going to resolve to pay off some plastic, you should consider these options:

Paying Down the Card That Is the Most "Maxed"

This is a credit score play, which is also an indirect financial play. Remember, every single one of your credit card issuers has the ability to check your credit reports as often as they like through a process called "account management." That means your spending activities on other cards are no secret and can lead to adverse creditor actions, even with the CARD Act protections in place.

Having a card that is highly leveraged often leads to lower credit scores because of your elevated utilization percentage. I wrote about utilization and how it's calculated earlier, in Chapter 10. Ignoring highly utilized cards can often lead to other credit card issuers increasing the interest rates on their cards, lowering their credit limits, or closing the account altogether. They're doing this because they can clearly see that you're bouncing near your credit limits, which is very indicative of elevated credit risk.

Paying Down the Card with the Lowest Balance

I'm not suggesting this strategy because you'll feel some sense of accomplishment when the statements stop coming, which may or may not actually be true. I'm suggesting it because it's also a credit score play, which comes with the same benefits as I described above.

There's a measurement in the FICO credit scoring system that counts the number of accounts with a balance greater than $0. In fact, for consumers who have decent scores, this is one of the more common reasons why their scores aren't even better. Eliminating a balance, or several of them, softens the blow of this measurement.

Paying Down the Card with the Lowest Interest Rate

This is a little counterintuitive, but still a solid strategy, especially if you do business with trigger-happy credit card issuers who haven't gotten their arms around their credit card default rates. The last thing you want to do is give your credit card issuer an incentive to increase your interest rate from 12.99 percent to 24.99 percent just because your balance is too high.

The CARD Act prevents retroactive rate increases, so it does them no financial good on the current balance to increase your rates. But if you've proven that you are willing to run up a huge balance on a low-rate card, then perhaps you'd be willing to do so on a card with a higher rate, where they will benefit financially. As long as your card is at least twelve months old, the issuer can increase your rate for any reason as long as they give you a forty-five-day advance notice.

Paying Down the Card with the Highest Limit

There are a variety of reasons why it's good to have high limits on your credit cards. Perhaps the most significant benefit is the access to unsecured capital, which in most cases costs you nothing more than maybe an annual fee. And, as previously mentioned, your credit scores benefit from having cards with high limits. You'd like to maintain these benefits by *not* giving your issuer incentive to lower your limits.

There is a phenomenon in the credit card industry called "chasing the balance," which became more commonly known after Hurricane Katrina. Many Gulf Coast residents were using their retail cards to survive, and many issuers of those cards were lowering the limits down to the current balance. When the cardholder made a payment, the issuer would lower the limit in lockstep, thus chasing the balance.

If your issuer feels like your risk has elevated, but not enough to close the card, they may either lower your limit by a predetermined percentage *or* chase your balance right down to when you pay it off. Keeping your balance moderate even on high-limit cards can prevent this.

You've probably noticed that most of these strategies are either contradictory or at least not always in the best interest of the issuer. Credit card issuer risk managers are tasked with controlling the downside risk of their cardholder portfolio, and they don't have all the answers. That's why your "risk" measurement is fluid from one issuer to another, and even from one billing cycle to another. Clear as mud, eh?

WHICH CREDIT CARDS SHOULD I CLOSE?

One of the most common questions I get has to do with the impact of closing credit cards: "Which card or cards should I close?" Most consumers are aware of the fact that closing credit cards can lower your credit scores, but that's really where the facts end and the fiction begins.

Sometimes the relentless pursuit of those great credit scores causes us to do things that might seem foolish. In some of the following situations, the smartest move might not be the best move for your credit scores. Please keep that in mind as you read on.

First and foremost, if you've conceded that you simply can't properly manage credit cards, then you shouldn't have them, period. But if you simply want to prune your wallet of some unused or expensive plastic, then there is a right way and a wrong way to go about it. Each strategy has its pros and cons.

The Most Financial Benefit

If you want to get the most financial bang for your buck, then rank your credit cards by their interest rates from highest to lowest and then slice off the top card(s). This strategy, which you didn't need to hear from me because it's so fundamental, is only useful if you revolve a balance from one month to the next. If you pay your cards off each month, then the interest rate is irrelevant.

The annual fee associated with a card can also seem to be a reason for closing it. But most annual fees are well below $100, so if you think about the other things you're spending money on, a credit card annual fee doesn't seem so bad. Having access to thousands of dollars of unsecured capital has value. Remember this before you close cards just because they have annual fees. You might regret your move.

The Most Credit Score Benefit

The above header is purposely deceptive. There is no credit score benefit to closing credit card accounts. When you close an account, you lose the value of the unused credit limit, which can really slam your scores. If you close credit cards that have a balance, the damage will be less than if you close cards that have no balance.

If you do choose to close accounts that have no balance, then choose the card with the lowest credit limit, which is probably going to be a retail store credit card (those will also likely have the highest interest rates). Or, alternatively, close charge cards since they have no credit limits and are not counted by newer scoring models in the infamous "debt utilization" category.

The Biggest Myth about Closing Credit Cards

Here goes . . . "Close the newest card, because if you close old cards, you'll lose the value of their age in your credit scores." No, no, no. That's incorrect. The only way you lose the value of an old account is if/when it's removed from your credit reports. As long as the account is still on your credit reports, then the scoring models see how old it is and your scores will continue to benefit from its age. The incorrect assumption is that credit-scoring models only look at open accounts when considering age-related factors.

The Fair Credit Reporting Act doesn't require the removal of closed accounts that are positive (void of negative information). We know at least one of the credit bureaus will allow a closed account to remain on file for ten or more years. Point being, when you're going through the process of choosing which accounts to close, don't worry about how old they are.

CHAPTER 16

Credit Cards, Charge Cards & Rewards Cards

Pick a card, almost any card, and you'll likely be holding some sort of rewards card. The rewards card has become almost ubiquitous among the various companies that issue plastic. Airline miles, points, cash, merchandise, discounts, gas, and concierge services are among the rewards or benefits you could realize in exchange for using certain cards for your spending needs.

REWARDS CARDS: WORTH THE PRICE?

But are the rewards really worth it? Should you instead be focusing your attention elsewhere, like on the terms of use or interest rates? Have the rewards become a strategy to distract us away from poor terms? And finally, is rewarding people for spending and likely getting into debt responsible or not? Shouldn't we be rewarded for paying off debt rather than getting into debt?

A quick survey of credit card websites reveals that rewards cards dominate the offerings. In fact, it's easier to find a rewards card than it is a card without some sort of rewards offering.

Debit card offerings have even gotten into the game by offering rewards programs.

I believe there are two groups of people who use rewards cards: those who use them strictly to pay for things they already would have purchased and those who spend to earn the reward. You might think the first group is in good shape with no possible downside to their use of plastic to pay for everything simply to get the rewards, and you'd be wrong. Charging everything possible just to earn the points and then paying it all off at the end of the month saves you from the interest, but it doesn't save you from the possible credit score damage of having higher utilization not only on that card but also, possibly, in aggregate. Both measurements are important in your credit scores.

The second group is a disaster waiting to happen. Anyone who buys and incurs debt simply to earn points or cash doesn't realize that rewards programs are largely structured to reward the issuer rather than the cardholder. Let me give you a very simple but shocking example about what it really costs to earn certain rewards.

American Express issues the Delta SkyMiles Card, which I have and use. For each dollar you spend, you get a mile. Once you earn enough miles you can redeem them for airfare, which on the surface sounds simple enough. And, in all fairness to that program, you do get 25,000 miles after your first purchase and other bulk mile-rewards after you meet certain spending thresholds such as "$10,000 in qualifying purchases on the card within six months."

The annual fee on that card is $150, so at the very least I know I'm going to pay $150 per year for this card. A round-trip ticket from Atlanta to LaGuardia (New York) with a sixty-day advance purchase is $198, and a round trip from Atlanta to Los Angeles with a sixty-day notice is as low as $261 (at the time this book went to print). Point being, you might be better off just buying a ticket at retail or via one of the discount websites.

Notwithstanding the bulk miles given to you when you sign up for that card, you'll have to spend at least $25,000 to earn enough miles (25,000) to pay for either of those two round-trip tickets, and that's if they're even available when you book your flights. If your ticket is more expensive than $250, then the redemption structure becomes fairly complicated, which brings me to my second point.

Rewards programs can get very complicated, very quickly. They can also expire, be scaled back, and even be fully withdrawn. This is why if you're going to sign up for a rewards program, I suggest that you choose one that gives you cash back or credits your account . . . and then redeem it as soon as possible. Cash-back programs are easy to understand and, most importantly, cash has no blackout dates.

Still, spending to earn the cash back makes no sense, either. Most of the cash programs reward you with $1 for every $100 you spend, or 1 percent. So the same airline tickets in my previous example would have cost $19,800 and $26,100 in spending to earn enough cash to buy the tickets outright . . . and those are inexpensive tickets.

And in the worst-case scenario, if you revolve a balance on a rewards card you'll quickly pay for your own reward, and then some. Follow my math: the average interest rate on a credit card is now 14.7 percent according to Synovate, which means if you charge even just $5,000 and pay the minimum payment each month (3 percent in this example), then you'll pay off the card in a whopping 174 months (assuming you don't incur any more debt) and pay over $3,300 in interest. But hey, at least you'll have earned 5,000 miles or $50 cash back.

In the best-case scenario, rewards cards should be used *only* if you will pay off the debt in full each month, which is how we should all be using credit cards anyway. And if you are a heavy user of the card each month, it's a good idea to look into a small-business rewards card rather than a personal rewards card. This way it's less likely that the debt will end up on your personal credit reports and you'll protect your scores.

Enjoy your flight!

CHARGE CARDS VERSUS CREDIT CARDS: YOU DECIDE

It's been the raging debate for decades: should I pay for that iPad with my charge card or with my credit card? OK, so I've exaggerated a bit on the history of the debate, but despite my sarcasm, it is a valid discussion. Which is the better slice of plastic, the charge card or the credit card?

As I like to do before I dive in, let's review the definition of each type of card.

A **charge card** looks exactly like a credit card in shape, size, and usability, but that's where the similarities end. Charge cards do not have credit limits, so theoretically you can charge as much as you want, until the issuer decides enough is enough. That's because, despite the lack of a credit limit, charge cards do have what's referred to as a shadow limit, which is the upper boundary of your capacity to charge. Also, charge cards must be paid in full each month, unless you have a hybrid card that allows you to choose to pay only some of the balance. Charge cards generally have annual fees because of the lack of interest income.

A **credit card** does have a credit limit, which is the preset upper boundary of your capacity to charge. Common credit limits for low-end credit cards can range from a few hundred dollars to a few thousand dollars. Limits for higher-end cards, normally carrying various names of precious metals, can be as high as ten, twenty, thirty thousand dollars or more. Credit cards do not have to be paid in full each month because you can "revolve" a balance from one month to the next. The price for this is the interest you pay on the unpaid debt. Credit cards don't generally have annual fees because of the interest income, but we're seeing more credit card issuers experimenting with annual fees on credit cards for those holders who don't generate much revenue.

The clear benefit of a charge card is the fact that you're less likely to get into crushing debt because you know that roughly twenty-one days after you receive your statement, you'll have to pay it in full. Charge cards are also a decent way to establish, build, and maintain solid credit histories and credit scores. Note my use of the word "decent."

The downside to charge cards, and it's not a huge downside, is the lack of a set credit limit. As I discussed in Chapter 10, an important factor in your FICO credit scores is what's referred to as utilization, which is the relationship between your balances and your credit limits expressed as a percentage. So, for example, a $1,000 balance on a credit card with a $10,000 credit limit equates to 10 percent utilization ($1,000/$10,000 = .1), which is very good. But in the absence of a credit limit, as in the case of a charge card, most credit and insurance scoring models will use the "high balance" as a substitute. And normally the high balance is lower than the credit limit.

So, if your high balance in a similar charge card example is only $2,000, then some scoring models will interpret you as being 50 percent utilized ($1,000/$2,000 = .5), and that's not good. In fairness to all involved, the newer versions of credit scoring models do not include charge cards in the utilization calculations, but not all lenders are using the newer versions of these models.

The downside to credit cards is the fact that you can get into a lot of debt in a short period of time. If you choose to revolve a balance from one month to the next while only making the minimum payment and continuing to use the card, you are headed for trouble. Credit cards are often abused by those who consider them as income rather than as a method of convenient shopping. The default rate on credit cards is north of 10 percent right now, which is troubling.

The upside to credit cards is the fact that they don't usually have annual fees and you can still pay them in full each month, just like a charge card. There is also the non-issue of the aforementioned credit score/credit limit/high balance dilemma, because most credit card issuers do, in fact, report your actual credit limit on your credit reports.

I personally have several of each card type in my wallet. I have them not because I like one type more than the other, but more so because of my profession: I have to test-drive these products if I want to write intelligently about them. Your best option is going to be based on how you plan on using the card. So choose wisely, my friends.

PART IV

Damage Control, Credit Repair & Debt Settlement Services

CHAPTER 17

Credit Repair & Debt Settlement

Both of these services are marketed as ways to either improve your credit or get you out of debt, or both. These services have fairly poor reputations, but are they really as evil as some would have you believe?

CREDIT REPAIR SERVICES: I WRITE, YOU DECIDE

The subject of credit repair is a powder keg, lightening rod, PR loser . . . choose your own metaphor. Opinions on the subject seem to be polarized, meaning you either like credit repair companies or you hate credit repair companies.

First off, what is a credit repair company? According to the Credit Repair Organizations Act (CROA), the federal law that defines how credit repair companies must do business, a credit repair company is actually referred to as a credit repair organization (or CRO). And a CRO is anyone who "sells, provides, or performs any service, in return for the payment of money or other valuable consideration, for the express or implied purpose of improving any consumer's credit record, credit history, or credit rating."

There are some exceptions to that rule. If you're a nonprofit and perform those duties, then you're not a CRO. If you're a bank or a credit union, then you're also not a CRO. But if you are for profit, aren't a bank, and sell services promising to help a consumer's credit, then you're a CRO—whether you want to be one or not.

There are people who believe all credit repair is illegal. That's not true. According to Edward Jamison, lawyer and founder of CreditCRM, a developer of credit repair business software, "Credit repair is anything but illegal if you do it the right way." And the "right way" means you fully comply with the requirements of CROA and any state equivalent. And how exactly do you comply with CROA? According to credit repair experts, CROA states that a CRO must do the following things, and others, in order to be in compliance:

- Provide mandatory disclosures letting consumers know, among other things, that they can dispute credit information directly with the credit bureaus.
- Avoid making any misleading or untrue statements about any consumer's creditworthiness. You can't say, "We guarantee we can remove your negative credit items."
- Avoid charging or receiving any money in advance of any services that have not been fully performed. You can't charge $100 for services that will be rendered over the next thirty days or you could become FTC roadkill.

Credit repair services dispute information on your credit reports in an effort to get negative items removed. The exact volume of disputes isn't known, but according to Stuart Pratt, president of the Consumer Data Industry Association (the trade organization of the credit reporting agencies), the volume represents "no less than 30 percent of disputes."

This dispute volume is accomplished, according to Pratt, by "flooding" the credit bureaus with dispute letters in an attempt to "break the system," thus resulting in the removal of the offending credit entry.

Further, according Pratt, "credit repair efforts most often end up in failure." However, on their website, credit repair company Lexington Law claims to have removed over one million items in 2009 alone, including collections, late payments, charge-offs, liens, bankruptcies, repossessions, foreclosures, and judgments. Given that the credit bureaus house over 200 million credit reports containing countless credit data items, that number represents a very small percentage as a whole of alleged errors, but might be very meaningful for Lexington Law's much smaller customer base. It, however, omits the fact that many of the items would have been removed anyway if the consumer attempted to have them removed on their own rather than paying a monthly subscription in exchange for credit repair services.

The credit industry has taken a beating thanks to CROA. In fact, both FICO and Equifax have settled class-action lawsuits alleging they violated the act. Does anyone honestly believe that FICO or Equifax is a credit repair organization? This has led to industry veterans, myself included, to call for a change in CROA so that it keeps the scam artists out of the industry, but allows for reputable companies to operate without fear of class-action lawsuits for negligible or technical violations. The act seems to be overly burdensome in its requirements that might have made sense when it went into effect in 1996, but not so much in 2012.

There is also a move among credit repair industry leadership to change how the players operate, so its long-tarnished reputation can be "repaired" (pardon the pun). According to Michael Citron, CEO of DisputeSuite, a developer of credit repair business software, "Most credit repair companies truly intend to do the right thing for consumers, and most are managed by good people." He did acknowledge that "there are some bad apples, as in any industry. However, in the credit repair industry the amount of propaganda in comparison to the truth is not even close."

Citron seems to be correct. According to the Federal Trade Commission, the organization tasked with enforcing CROA, only 2 percent of their complaints are specific to "Advance-Fee Loans and Credit Protection/Repair," and given the increase in advance-fee loan scams, the 2 percent figure can't be attributed only to credit repair. To put this in perspective, the FTC receives over 250 percent more complaints about Internet auctions than it receives about credit repair and over 350 percent more complaints about lotteries.

So whether you like or dislike credit repair companies, their services are not flat-out illegal, they don't seem to be blatantly dishonest about their effectiveness, and they aren't dominating the complaint line at the FTC. But you might very well be able to do what they do on your own.

There, now you pick a side! I'm Switzerland.

TRYING TO GET OUT OF CREDIT CARD DEBT? WHAT YOU SHOULD KNOW ABOUT DEBT SETTLEMENT COMPANIES

Everyone knows the story. Unemployment is up. FICO scores are down for many consumers. Home values are down. And because home values are down, home equity has disappeared for millions of homeowners. And since home equity was the financial safety net millions of consumers used to pay off their credit card debt, well, you know the rest. Let's just agree that millions of consumers have no way to pay off all of their credit card debt right now.

There are a variety of ways to get out of credit card debt, right? You can budget your way out of debt. You can file bankruptcy. You can enroll in a debt management plan (DMP) through one of the member organizations of the National Foundation for Credit Counseling, commonly referred to as Consumer Credit Counseling Service (CCCS). You can work with your credit card issuer directly and seek help through one of their hardship programs. You can attempt to settle the debt on your own. Or you can enlist the services of a debt settlement company.

Opinions vary on these options. They all have their pros and cons. The purpose here isn't to explore each option. The purpose of this is to explore debt settlement as an option.

Settlement is quite an easy concept to understand. You agree to pay your credit card issuer an amount of money less than what you really owe them, and they consider the debt to be paid in full. So, if you owe John's Bank $10,000 and I agree to accept $5,000 as "full payment," then you have settled your debt with John's Bank. The bank reports the settlement to the credit reporting agencies and sends you a 1099 for the forgiven amount. Settlement, incidentally, is considered one of FICO's seven deadly sins in terms of damage to your credit score (covered back in Chapter 11).

Settlement can be accomplished by working directly with your bank. You do not have to hire someone to do this for you. That's a myth. In fact, many credit card issuers won't even work with debt settlement companies, so you have no choice but to deal with them directly. This is all right, because all creditors have their version of a "remediation" department, which is where you'll likely end up if you call them asking for a settlement deal.

Now, let's move on to the debt settlement companies. You've all seen their commercials. Distraught couples staring at their credit card statements magically turning into happy families playing with puppies in their front yard, all thanks to the friendly ol' debt settlement company. Heck, there's even a version that has excerpts from one of President Obama's speeches, and a picture of a government building in the background. It's clearly intended to come across as a government program. Of course, it's not a government program.

Here's how they work. First, they find out how much debt you have. This is to determine if you're even worth doing business with. If you have too little debt, then they won't make enough money working with you. That's why their ads contain statements like "If you have more than $10,000 in credit card debt, call now. . . ." If you have enough debt, in their eyes, then they'll sign you up.

When you sign up, they'll tell you to stop communicating with your credit card issuers. I'm not kidding, they really tell you this. That means no more payments and no more return calls. The hypothesis here is to get your credit card issuer so desperate for payment that they'll accept a settlement offer.

At the same time, you'll be asked to make monthly payments to the settlement company. Why? Because you're creating a war chest that serves two purposes. First, this is where their fees will come from. Second, this is where the settlement offer will come from.

After several months, or longer, there will be enough money for them to make some sort of offer to the credit card issuer. The issuer may accept the offer, or they may decline the offer. Either way, your fees to the settlement company have been paid.

So what happens during the period of time when you're paying the debt settlement company (and ignoring your creditors)? Well, since that's not a part of the commercials, I'll have to be the one who breaks the bad news.

- Your credit will be trashed. The credit card issuer will report the ascending level of late payments to the credit bureaus, which remain on your credit file for seven years. Now, the debt settlement guys will say, "Well, your credit is probably already trashed, so no big deal." Wrong. New (and numerous) late payments help to lock in lower scores for additional time. And it gets worse . . .

- The card issuer will likely enlist the services of a third-party collection agency to collect the debt. This means a brand-new collection will be reported to your credit files. Again, this remains for seven years. And these guys can pull your credit reports to find you and determine your ability to pay them. That means you'll have to explain collection inquiries. You're supposed to ignore these guys, as well. And it gets worse . . .

- That knock at your door . . . yeah, that guy is called a process server. Your credit card company, or a collection attorney, has sued you for nonpayment of the debt. You can't ignore him like you've been ignoring your credit card issuer. If you do choose to ignore the summons, you'll lose by default for not showing up to court. This is called a default judgment. And yes, the judgment can show up on your credit report for seven years. And it gets worse . . .

- Become familiar with the term "Writ of Sequestration." In English, this is either legal garnishment of your wages or seizure of your assets. If your wages are garnished, your employer will now be made aware of your defaulted debt problems because they're the ones who will hold back a portion of your salary.

You've totally lost control of the situation because you chose to ignore your creditors, at the request of a company trying to profit off of your debt situation. Smart? Or not?

And, just to tie a nice bow on the top of this one, the attorneys general in the states of Florida and Alabama have shut down major debt settlement networks because, and I quote, "they're a scam because consumers get no value for their fees."

CHAPTER 18

Mortgage Loan Modification, Short Sales & Time-Barred Debts

Loan modifications and short sales have become a popular way out of bad mortgage debts, but they can have a negative impact to your credit. But all debts do eventually become time barred, meaning the lender can no longer sue you for collection of the debt.

THE DOWNSIDE TO MORTGAGE LOAN MODIFICATIONS

Three years ago the term "loan modification" was practically unheard of, especially in the mortgage environment. Today, however, the term is almost as common as "refinance" and "home equity loan," and that's not necessarily a good thing. In this chapter we'll explore the loan modification option, as well as its credit downside.

A mortgage loan modification, hereafter described as a "loan mod," is the process whereby a mortgage lender will either temporarily or permanently modify the terms of a mortgage loan so the homeowner can continue to afford their payments, and thus stay in their home. A loan mod can be as simple as a reduction in the interest rate, or as extensive as a reduction of the balance owed. Either way, the net result is a lower payment for the homeowner.

The primary government program used to facilitate loan mods is HAMP (Home Affordable Modification Program), which is part of the Making Home Affordable program. The prospect of reworking the terms of your mortgage loan to make the payments more affordable sounds like a fantastic option for struggling homeowners. However, there is a significant credit downside to even attempting to modify your home loan.

When you apply for a loan modification, it's just that: an application. The lender decides whether or not you qualify for a modification based on your personal situation, including what kind of hardship you're suffering. Point being, you may think you have a hardship significant enough to warrant a loan mod, but the lender may disagree with you. But, of course, neither of you will know this until you apply for the modification.

If you do choose to apply, then you'll likely be asked to make a lower payment than normal during a "trial payment period." It's unknown what the logic is behind the lower monthly payment, other than to prove to the lender that you can successfully pay less than you're currently paying. The problem with these lower payments is that they don't satisfy your monthly minimum obligation. This means late payments will be reported to the credit bureaus, and you will start to incur late fees. And finally, each month your loan will become further and further past due.

The trial payment period is supposed to last only three months, which is more than enough time to process a loan mod application. The problem is many loan mod applications are taking six to nine months to process because of workforce reductions over the past three years. This means your lower (and late) payments will persist the entire time your trial period lasts. All the while, these late payments are driving your credit scores further and further down, or locking in already low scores for seven more years.

If your loan mod application is denied, you will be asked to immediately bring your payments current. This will include all balances in arrears plus late fees. This will likely be thousands of dollars because of the lengthy trial period. If you're unable to bring your payments current, your lender will begin foreclosure proceedings. And, of course, all of this will be reported to the credit reporting agencies for years to come.

The bottom line about loan modifications is that the hypothesis is solid. Lower payments should equal fewer defaults and more families remaining in their homes. However, the execution of the plan has so far been very poor, and consumers and their credit reports and scores have been caught in the middle.

THE TRUTH ABOUT SHORT SALES AND THEIR IMPACT ON YOUR CREDIT

One of the most frightening titles you can have right now is "homeowner." That's because millions of us have completely lost the equity in our homes, which means we are in the unenviable position of owing more than the home is actually worth. Nobody asks for their home's value to fall, but millions of homeowners are now in the position of trying to dispose of mortgages that are considered upside-down.

There are various ways to do this. First, you can actually find someone willing to buy your house for enough dough to cover all of the mortgages it secures. NOTE: That's probably not going to happen, so proceed to Option 2. Option 2 is to pay the difference out of your own pocket. So, if you owe $150,000 and find a buyer at $125,000, you'd have to show up at closing with a check for $25,000 to cover the difference. If that's not an option, then you can walk away from the home (foreclosure), turn the keys back over to the lender (forfeiture of deed in lieu of foreclosure), attempt to have the loan modified and stay in the property, or attempt to short sell the home.

A short sale is when the lender accepts less than the full loan balance and considers the loan to be paid. So, in the afore-mentioned example, if the lender had accepted $125,000 as a full payoff, then you would have been on your way to a success-ful short sale. The lender would eat the $25,000 deficiency and everyone would call it a day. But it's not that simple. There's the impact this event will likely have on your credit.

Short sales are a relatively new phenomenon, and because of this there's an incredible amount of misinformation about the impact they have on your credit. Some people are even going so far as to say that a short sale is neutral to your credit, which is incorrect. Short sales are reported to the credit reporting agencies as either settlements or charge-offs, both of which are accurate. The lender is settling for less than you really owe, and they're likely charging off the deficiency.

Some people, real estate agents in particular, have seized this reporting format to mean that short sales are not reported to the credit bureaus at all simply because the words "short" and "sale" do not show up on your credit reports. And they're using it to market the value of short sales as being a benign event in an effort to drum up business. Pretty much every rep-utable credit source acknowledges that short sales are just as bad for your credit as any other negative mortgage event, but just in case it's at all unclear, I offer the following statements from the people who actually invented the FICO credit score:

> "Both short sales and foreclosures are considered negative by the score, because our data shows us it's very predictive of future credit risk. The claim that doing a

short sale is not going to hurt your score is false. It's inaccurate."

—Tom Quinn, former vice president of
FICO scores at Fair Isaac Corp
(*Minneapolis Star Tribune*)

"To the FICO score, there is very little difference between a short sale, a deed-in-lieu, or a foreclosure— and we've been saying that to anybody who will listen, but this rumor that short sales are somehow benign has persisted."

—Craig Watts, a spokesman for Fair Isaac,
the maker of FICO scores
(*American Banker*)

That should just about clear up any misunderstanding or misrepresentation of how a short sale affects your credit. It's still a better option than a foreclosure, because people trying to market their home for a short sale will still maintain the home's cleanliness, mow the lawn, and won't rip out the copper piping or appliances. But it's still not a clean break between you and your mortgage lender.

TIME-BARRED DEBTS: HOW LONG CAN YOU BE SUED FOR A BAD DEBT?

"Statute of limitations" refers to the amount of time that can pass after some sort of event before legal actions regarding that event can no longer be initiated. For example, in the credit world, if you incurred some sort of contractual debt in the state of California and defaulted, you couldn't be sued for collection after four years. After the statute of limitations has expired, that debt becomes a "time-barred debt," meaning the lender's ability to sue you for collection has passed.

Now, don't get me wrong. I'm not talking about the amount of time it can be reported to the credit bureaus, and I'm not talking about the amount of time the lender or collection agency has to collect on the debt. "Time barred" just refers to when the court loses the ability to legally force you to pay.

Here's the straight info on time-barred contract debts:

If you lived in this state when you incurred the contract debt . . .	. . . then this is how many years the collector has to sue you
DE, MD, MS, NC, NH, SC, DC	3
CA, PA, TX	4
FL, ID, NE, OK, RI, VA	5
AL, AK, AZ, AR, CO, CT, GA, HI, KS, ME, MA, MI, MN, NV, NJ, NM, NY, ND, OR, SD, TN, UT, VT, WA, WI	6
MT	8
IL, IN, IA, LA, MO, WV, WY	10
KY, OH	15

It's important to point out that where you lived when you incurred the debt *may* take precedence over where you currently live. "Generally speaking, the statute of limitations of the state where the contract was formed will control if the contract is silent on the issue," according to Sean P. Flynn, Esq., a former shareholder with Ropers, Majeski, Kohn & Bentley, PC, a law firm that represents defendants in Fair Debt Collection and Fair Credit Reporting litigation in California and New York. If you signed a contract with a bank while you lived in Mississippi, but then moved to Ohio, then the statute of limitations could be based on Mississippi law. And that's good news, because you can be sued for only three years in Mississippi versus fifteen years in Ohio.

Here's the straight info on how long defaulted debts can be reported to the credit reporting agencies ... pretty simple:

The state you lived in when you incurred the debt	The # of years a creditor or collector can report the item in your credit report
All 50, plus DC	7

When Do You *Not* Pay Your Bill?

If the collector can't sue you for payment any longer, then do you really need to pay the debt? I would argue that you should always pay your obligations as long as you're really the one who owes it. And just because they can't sue you, doesn't mean they can't report it to the credit bureaus. Having a paid-off debt is better than having an unpaid debt. In fact, some creditors will require that you pay off collections before they'll do business with you, regardless of your credit scores or the age of the debt.

Will Creditors Really Sue Me for Non-Payment?

The short answer is "yes." The better answer is "If you owe a creditor more than $1,000 in defaulted debt and you're ignoring them, then you stand the risk of being sued." The higher the dollar amount, the higher your odds of getting sued. A fantastic proxy for "collection aggression" is the number of FDCPA (Fair Debt Collection Practices Act) and FCRA (Fair Credit Reporting Act) lawsuits filed *against* collectors and creditors for (allegedly) illegally attempting to collect debts and the reporting of those debts to consumer credit bureaus. According to Jack Gordon, president of Michigan-based WebRecon, a company that tracks FDCPA and FCRA lawsuits, "there were 12,159 FDCPA and FCRA lawsuits filed in 2010. That's a record number."

What this means is collectors were very aggressive in 2010 and there's really nothing to indicate that they'll calm down in the next year or two. And while many of the above-mentioned lawsuits are baseless shakedowns of collection agencies, it's no secret that collectors have become more industrious with their tactics, including litigation.

CHAPTER 19

Student Loan Debt

In October 2011, *USA Today* sent a message that many of you needed to hear years ago. They indicated that student loan debt had passed $1 trillion, which is an increase from the $830 billion figure published by the *Wall Street Journal* in August 2010, when student loan debt officially passed credit card debt. It seems like irresponsibility has jumped the track and now resides in the classroom. This is reckless spending in the name of education. I've often been accused of not sugarcoating my financial opinions and this will be no different. Here's why I'm often the most unpopular guy in the room. Buckle up.

STUDENT LOAN DEBT PASSES CREDIT CARD DEBT: MY EXTREMELY UNPOPULAR PERSPECTIVE

Tuition is a product, plain and simple. And just like any other product, you have to be responsible with your choices. Do you buy a Mercedes Benz when you can only afford a Hyundai? Do you buy a $1,000,000 home when you can only afford a $150,000 townhouse? Then why in the world would you ever let your eighteen-year-old kid, who is no longer allowed to get a measly credit card on his or her own, walk blindly down the path of financial suicide just to go to an expensive school?

I'm about to give you the tough love your parents didn't give you. And I realize it might be too late for you, but ignoring this doesn't stop the cycle. Here's the bottom line on this issue: it's easier **not** to get into this debt than it is to deal with the debt once you're in it. As of today, you can't discharge government-guaranteed student loans in bankruptcy. That means you **will** pay it back, even if it takes the rest of your life.

Think About Community College for Your Core

You don't need to take English 101 and Chemistry 101 at Duke. You can take them at a community college or a state school and then transfer. Your core curriculum doesn't need to cost you the same as your final two or three years. This is like paying the same amount for preseason NFL tickets as you do for regular season games. And yes, I know some schools won't let you transfer those core credits, but many will.

Brown, Stanford, Duke? Come On!

Why won't you be reasonable with your college choices just like you should be reasonable with every other credit decision? No, you don't need to go to Brown at $50,000 per year. No, you don't need to go to Notre Dame at $40,000 per year. No, you don't need to drive that new BMW. No, you don't need to run up $20,000 in credit card debt. Is there really a difference? There's nothing wrong with an in-state state school, with community college for your core. Going to an expensive school isn't a birthright, and parents who sit on their tongues and let their kids head down this "expensive is better" path are 100 percent to blame.

College Degree, Reality Check!

Parents and advisors need to step up and give their kids, who don't know any better at eighteen, a dose of reality about college degrees, which are basically nothing more than an "entry pass" to the bigger job market. You don't need a fancy five-year degree (and maybe even grad school) that ends up costing you $100,000 in student loans unless there's real ROI at graduation (law, medicine, nursing . . . something that pays off and practically guarantees you a job for as long as you want one). Choose a degree that gets you in the workforce door and be done with it. If you're still depending on your degree to get a job five years after you graduate, then you're not doing well. Experience is the real selling point eventually. I'm quite certain I've never been hired because of my impressive BS in Criminal Justice from the University of West Georgia.

The Path

Just like frugal car buyers never buy a new car and always get something that simply solves the "point A to point B" problem, so you should take a frugal approach to a college education. And cheaper doesn't equate to substandard, so don't swallow that pill. There is absolutely nothing wrong with community college for your core and a state school for your major.

HOW STUDENT LOANS AFFECT YOUR CREDIT

Last year total outstanding student loan debt surpassed credit card debt in the United States. Those of you with student loans are collectively in over $1 trillion of debt. And unlike credit card debt, most student loan debt will hang out with you until you pay it—or you die.

As an expert in the credit industry, I frequently write for online publications. After writing about the number of credit scores that we all have (which I covered earlier in Chapter 6) for the good folks at Mint.com, a reader named Grant commented on my post and asked a variety of questions about how student loans affect your scores, and how best to deal with them. His timing and his questions were so excellent that it warranted a full feature. So, thanks to Grant for submitting the following questions:

Question: Can paying off student loans early hurt your credit score due to the length of the loan?

Answer: No. This is a common credit-scoring myth. Paying off your loans early doesn't have any impact on the age or "length" of the loan. A loan opened three years ago is still three years ago regardless of whether or not it's paid off, paid off early, or still unpaid.

Question: Can paying student loans early hurt your credit score, since banks want the full amount of interest?

Answer: No. The banks don't control your credit scores like that, so they can't harm your score because they're not getting the full amount of interest. Further, the amount of interest you pay (or don't pay) is not reported to the credit bureaus, so it's systemically impossible for it to have any influence on your credit scores.

Question: Can paying off your student loans early hurt your scores because of the decrease in the average age of accounts?

Answer: No. The answer to this question is essentially the same as the first one. The average age of your accounts, which is important to your scores, includes both open and closed accounts. As such, paying any loan off early (and then closing the account, if it's a credit card) has no negative influence on the average age of your accounts or your credit scores.

Question: Can student loans be reported in "triplicate," so one loan looks like three loans?

Answer: This is a possibility. Student loans are often reported on a disbursement by disbursement basis. So, if you're in school for four years and you get one student loan per year, or per quarter, or per semester . . . each of those disbursements of funds can be reported as a unique loan on your credit reports. So, if you have eight loans over four years, yes, it can show up eight times on your credit reports.

Question: Does consolidating student loans help your scores?

Answer: It certainly can. If you can eliminate multiple accounts on your credit reports and replace them with only one loan, albeit for the full aggregate amount, then you'll likely improve your scores because you've eliminated several accounts with a balance.

Question: Does it make sense to pay off the smaller loans faster to reduce the number of loans?

Answer: Most certainly. If you've got small loans and larger loans and you can knock out the smaller loans without compromising things like savings and emergency funds, then go for it. It will eliminate accounts that have balances, which is always a good thing for your credit scores.

NOTE: The strategy to increase your scores by eliminating accounts with balances will work if you can pay off small credit card balances as well. Some people use multiple retail store cards and run up small nuisance balances because they think they have to use the store's card instead of a general use credit card for all of their purchases. You can just as easily use a general use credit card (Visa, Mastercard, Discover, Amex) for all of your purchases instead of a Gap Card at the Gap, a Macy's Card at Macy's, etc.

PART V

Insurance, Massive Data Breaches & Identity Theft

CHAPTER 20

Insurance & Credit Reports

Section 604 of the Fair Credit Reporting Act says that the credit reporting agencies—Equifax, Experian, and TransUnion—may furnish reports to any company that intends to use that information for the purpose of underwriting insurance. So at the federal level, the use of credit reports for underwriting insurance is perfectly legal and many insurance companies do so. The real question is: why do they do it?

WHY DO INSURANCE COMPANIES USE CREDIT REPORTS AND CREDIT SCORES?

Insurance companies have the same issues lenders have—understanding the risk of doing business with certain consumers. It's not necessarily the risk of being paid or not being paid for their services (premiums). It's more the risk of providing a policy for someone who is more likely to file claims and thus be a less profitable customer. Yes, it's all about the money.

The primary difference between banking and insurance is that insurance policies are all secured, essentially. If you don't pay your premiums, they'll cut you off, which could lead to you losing your home (it's called a non-monetary default) or you getting arrested for driving without insurance. Determining whether or not you'll pay your premiums is not the primary reason some of them pull your credit reports and credit scores.

The primary reason is to determine if they even want to do business with you and/or under what terms. Despite what many believe, how you manage your credit is very predictive of what kind of insurance customer you'll be. It's predictive not only of your likelihood of filing claims, but also predictive of how profitable you'll be. If it weren't, then insurance companies wouldn't spend the money buying millions of credit reports and scores each year.

Not the Same Credit Scores

Much like the financial services environment, the insurance environment relies heavily on credit scores. This isn't anything new. However, the type of score they're using is not the same type of score banks and other financial services companies use. In fact, they're very different.

The scores used by insurance companies are called Insurance Credit Bureau Scores or Insurance Risk Credit Scores. They are developed by a variety of companies, including FICO and LexisNexis. LexisNexis develops the LexisNexis Attract Score, which is very commonly used by insurance companies.

Insurance scores consider credit information and/or previous insurance claim information. So, if you filed an auto claim or a homeowner's claim, it can be considered in your insurance score and it can result in a lower score. And if you're assuming the presence of claims means you're a less profitable insurance customer, well, you'd be right. Again, it's all about the money.

The Same Credit Reports

While the scores used by insurance companies are different, the reports they use are the same as the reports used by financial services companies. The reason? All credit reports originate from the same three places: Equifax, Experian, and TransUnion. Point being, there are no secret credit reports that insurance companies use to set your premiums.

Insurance Inquiries Don't Hurt Your Credit Scores

Enough bad news . . . time for some good news. When you apply for insurance, the insurance company may or may not access your credit reports and scores. There is no guarantee that they will, in fact, pull your credit reports. But it's a safe bet.

If the insurance company does choose to access your credit report and score, there will be an inquiry posted to the credit file. It will clearly be identified as being from your insurance company. And, more importantly, it will systemically be coded as coming from an insurance company. This is good news because insurance-related inquiries are not counted in your credit scores.

You will be able to see them, but no other entity will be able to see them. And credit-scoring systems don't consider insurance-related inquiries, so they'll never lower your credit scores.

I'll end on that high note.

CHAPTER 21

Data Breaches & Identity Theft

If you think you've protected yourself from identity theft, you're wrong. Your data is being maintained by hundreds of different companies, and they're all targets for data breaches and hacks. We can only do so much to protect ourselves.

DATABASES HACKED, YOUR IDENTITY JACKED!

It seems we can't go more than a few weeks without our personal information being compromised by a massive data breach: the New York Yankees, the Sony PlayStation network (twice and maybe thrice), Epsilon. All of these high-profile data breaches have one thing in common: we had nothing to do with it.

If you believe some of the credit bureaus' marketing ads, we're all just one step away from living in our parents' basement, working at fast food restaurants, having our credit reports and scores trashed, and even being falsely arrested. The FTC's top consumer complaint in 2010 (for the eleventh year straight) was identity theft. The marketing push seems to be parallel to the statistics, but really, other than buying a bunch of credit monitoring services, what are we supposed to do?

We've all heard the tired advice from experts (including this one) about how to avoid being an identity theft victim. Shred your sensitive documents instead of just throwing them away. Check your credit reports several times each year. And beware of phishing, vishing, spear phishing, skimming, RFID hacking, dumpster diving, and mail theft. You need a separate dictionary just to understand all of the ways these dirtbags are trying to scam you.

Other than shredding sensitive documents, making sure your mail doesn't sit in your box too long, checking your credit reports from time to time, making sure your passwords are complex, and using a little advanced common sense (no, you don't have a friend stuck in the UK looking for $2,000 to come home), we should be pretty safe from identity thieves. But what if mega-companies who are entrusted with our sensitive information are not good stewards of the data? Seriously, what's more likely to happen: someone stealing old checkbook registers from your garbage or Sony being hacked?

It's an unsolvable problem, because you can't remove yourself from "the system." Think about how many places maintain your sensitive information: frequent flyer accounts, your tax prep services, your CPA, hotel chains, retailers, banks, brokerage firms, newspapers, employers, credit card issuers, home owners' associations, insurance companies, airline clubs, domain registrars, public utilities, Facebook, Twitter, LinkedIn, Myspace, email service providers . . . our data is everywhere. Look at the list of bookmarks in your browser. How many of those places have your information? Almost all of them, I bet.

We certainly can't exit the system and we certainly can't expect companies to be impenetrable. What we can do is be a little less lazy about our log-in credentials, for example. We tend to use the same log-in credentials for multiple online accounts. That makes the Sony breach problematic because log-in credentials might have been stolen.

And it's not just credit card numbers or log-in credentials that put us at risk. Take the Epsilon breach, for example. You've probably never heard of Epsilon, but they manage email campaigns for scores of companies to the tune of about sixty million email addresses. And I'm not talking about John's Garage. I'm talking about Chase, TiVo, Best Buy, Disney, Marriott, Hilton, Citigroup, Ameriprise, and dozens of other widely recognized companies.

The hackers now have email addresses for millions of consumers, which makes spear phishing (email fraud perpetrated on a homogenous group) a possibility. To make matters worse, the people who hacked the Epsilon database are criminals, but they're not stupid criminals. They know the heat is on and the value on the data black market is less than what it will be in two years when everyone has forgotten about Epsilon.

The bottom line is we're vulnerable, both in the electronic and physical worlds. And regardless of how much time we spend running documents through shredders, there will always be exposure. I'm afraid the best we can do is to make ourselves a little less attractive than our neighbors by being smarter and more careful than they are.

Gotta run, I just got an email from TiVo telling me my service is going to get cut off unless I confirm my credit card information at their site. It's a good thing they sent me a link in their email. Now, where's my wallet?

IDENTITY THEFT PROTECTION: DO YOU KNOW YOUR OPTIONS?

When it comes to protecting your credit from identity theft, you have a variety of options. You can do nothing. You can pay to monitor your credit reports. Or you can freeze your credit reports. Each has their pros and cons, as more fully described below.

Do Nothing

I didn't include "do nothing" to be funny, even though I like my writing to have some sense of humor. The vast majority of people, in fact, do nothing to protect their identity, which doesn't necessarily mean they're at greater risk of being a target. The fact that you *have* an identity means you're a target, and even the most diligent shredder of personal documents is still just as much of a target as someone who dumps their tax returns in the garbage.

Even people who do nothing enjoy significant protections under the Fair Credit Reporting Act (FCRA), the Fair Credit Billing Act (FCBA), and the Electronic Fund Transfer Act (EFTA). The FCRA mandates that the credit reporting agencies add fraud alerts, provide free credit reports, and block information resulting from identity theft. The FCBA is the law that limits your liability for credit card theft to no more than $50, and the EFTA is the law that limits, somewhat, your liability if your debit or ATM cards are stolen and fraudulently used.

Credit Monitoring

Credit monitoring is a service offered by the credit reporting agencies and a small number of other companies. These services are almost always offered for a fee (either monthly or annual). They are very high-margin, which is why they're the primary service being sold by the credit bureaus and other companies online, and via their television advertising.

Credit monitoring is often referred to as being a "reactive" approach to identity theft protection because something bad has to happen to your credit reports before you're notified. Monitoring doesn't really prevent the fraud from occurring. It just hopes to notify you soon enough after the fraud has occurred to prevent any real damage.

Monitoring services look for credit report changes or additions that could be indicative of fraud. An addition of a new address, a new account, or new inquiries will likely set off monitoring alerts. Most of the alerts are either text message or email based. And most of the better (and more expensive) credit monitoring services will monitor all three of your credit reports daily.

Credit Freezes

Credit freezing is a service offered by the credit reporting agencies and other companies that gives consumers the ability to lock out access to their credit reports. According to Scott Mitic, CEO and founder of TrustedID, a consumer identity theft protection company, "Today any consumer in the United States can freeze their credit reports, but there is variance from state to state on what you will pay to do so."

Most credit experts believe a credit freeze is the best way to protect your credit reports from unauthorized access, primarily because it's proactive rather than reactive. Only lenders with whom you have an existing relationship will have access to your credit reports. Lenders with whom you have no relationship will not be able to access your credit reports unless you have thawed them in advance. "A credit freeze is the Fort Knox of credit protection" according to Mitic. "There simply is no stronger way to protect yourself from the most dangerous forms of identity theft."

Credit freezes are available in pretty much every state, thanks to state laws. And in many states, freezes are free for consumers who have been victims of identity theft. To see if you live in a state that mandates free credit freezes for identity theft victims, go to www.consumersunion.org/campaigns/learn_more/003484indiv.html.

PART VI

Credit Laws & Proposed Legislation

CHAPTER 22

FACTA's Free Annual Credit Reports

Since the beginning of 2004, Americans have had the right to claim their credit reports from each of the credit reporting agencies once every twelve months, for free. We were conferred this right by FACTA, which is the Fair and Accurate Credit Transactions Act of 2003. The methods (web, mail, phone) for claiming our free credit reports can be found at the website www.AnnualCreditReport.com. Have you ever claimed your free credit reports?

WHY AREN'T WE CLAIMING OUR FREE CREDIT REPORTS?

According to the Consumer Data Industry Association (CDIA), the trade organization of the credit reporting agencies, 175 million free credit reports have been claimed since the beginning of 2004, which averages out to 25 million free credit reports per year. At first glance, that sounds like a huge number, but when you break it down, you quickly realize that it's just a small percentage of how many could have been claimed. Follow my math.

There are three recognized national credit reporting agencies—Equifax, Experian, and TransUnion. All three of these credit reporting agencies house well over 200 million consumer credit files. This means collectively they hold at least 600 million credit files, which means there are at least 600 million credit files that can be claimed every twelve months.

The FACTA free credit report requirement has been in place for seven years now, which means 4.2 billion credit reports could have been claimed for free since the law took effect: 175 million is 4.16 percent of 4.2 billion. An easier way to figure out the percentage is to divide 25 million (the annual free haul) by 600 million.

The actual percentage is likely lower than 4.16 for a variety of reasons. The 4.16 percent calculation assumes that all of the Big Three (Equifax, Experian, and TransUnion) house exactly 200 million credit files. We know the number is actually much larger, but the bureaus won't disclose the exact number. And we aren't even counting the volume from the fourth credit bureau, Innovis Data Solutions, which is smaller than that of the Big Three, but still very significant. Point being, we're simply not taking advantage of our free credit report rights, and even 4.16 percent is probably a liberal figure.

The percentage is dreadful considering how important your credit is to getting a loan, insurance, or a job. The question is: why aren't we claiming our freebies? Here are some thoughts:

Consumer Apathy

Do we not care? Or is it that we don't care until we've been denied a loan or a job because of our credit? It seems to be on our New Year's resolution list every single year: improve our credit. Unfortunately, like "lose twenty pounds," that resolution seems to be forgotten by the time February rolls around.

Fear of What's There

Do you not want to know? "I believe some people just can't bear to look at their credit reports because they know they've screwed up," says Linda Sherry, director of national priorities for San Francisco–based Consumer Action. Her hypothesis makes perfect sense.

Consumers Don't Know Their Rights

In 2004, the media was all over the West Coast-to-East Coast implementation of the free credit report rule. California and other West Coast states were given the right first, and throughout the year the free report right moved east. During that year, it seemed as if AnnualCreditReport.com was written about almost daily. Unfortunately, the coverage has all but died save a few mentions here and there.

Confusion Caused by Aggressive "Free" Marketing of Credit Reports and Scores

If you own a television, then you've all seen the advertising for free credit reports and scores. Squirrels, Ben Stein, and really bad bands. Yeah, I guess I can see how all of that relates to credit. All of these companies blanket the airwaves and Internet with advertising for free credit reports and scores: FREECreditReport.com, FREECreditScore.com, FREETripleScore.com, FREEScore.com; none of these are actually free, but they *all* have the word "free" in their domains and advertising. And ironically, the one legitimate website for claiming your free annual credit reports does not have the word "free" in the domain.

Don't get me wrong. This isn't the credit bureaus' fault. It's not their job to stick a free credit report in your back pocket when you're not looking. The law requires them to be reactive, not proactive. It's up to us to ask for our reports and we're simply not doing a good job of it.

CHAPTER 23

Shoe Box Credit under the Equal Credit Opportunity Act

How familiar are you with Regulation B of the Equal Credit Opportunity Act (ECOA)? Wait, wait! Don't stop reading because I threw out an unfamiliar legal reference. What I'm about to tell you will forever change how you think about applying for credit.

THE BEST-KEPT SECRET IN LENDING

When you walk into a financial institution and apply for some sort of credit, you have to fill out an application. That application contains language giving the lender permission to pull your credit reports and scores. This gives them what's referred to in the Fair Credit Reporting Act (FCRA) as *permissible purpose* to get your credit data.

The lender pulls your credit reports and scores. Then they use that information to determine if they want to approve your application and under what terms. If they approve you, then you're welcomed into the family.

If, however, they deny your application, then you're sent on your merry way empty-handed, and a week or so later you get the rejection letter in the mail. That letter is called a "Notice of Adverse Action" and it provides you with notice of your right to get a free copy of the credit report the lender used to reject your application, and since July 22, 2011, that notice will also include the score they used to deny you. You can either claim your free credit report or you can do what most people do, which is nothing.

What I just described happens tens of thousands of times every single day. It has become the typical process of applying for credit. In fact, it has become so common that almost nobody knows that we, the applicants, actually are forgoing a very significant right.

Shoebox Credit

OK, back to Regulation B of the ECOA. Reg B requires that creditors, when evaluating the creditworthiness of an applicant, consider *any* information an applicant presents that reflects the applicant's creditworthiness. Further, at the request of the applicant (that's you), creditors *must* consider credit information not reported through a credit bureau if it's a similar type of credit account that they would consider if it were to be reported through a credit bureau.

I know that was a little confusing. Here's the lowdown: if you walk into a bank and apply for a loan and you hand the lender a shoebox full of receipts proving that you pay rent, cable, cell phone, insurance, electric power, natural gas, or any other credit obligation, they *must* consider it, per ECOA Reg B. What does that mean to you? It means you better go find a shoebox.

If you didn't know all of that, don't feel bad. Almost nobody knows their rights under Reg B. In fact, so few people know it that the National Credit Reporting Association says that they believe "ECOA Reg B has been conveniently forgotten by both the industry and the regulators at a cost to many credit-challenged consumers."

"ECOA Reg B provides every American with the federally protected right to build a credit history and credit score simply by paying everyday accounts on time, such as cell phone bills, rent, and utilities," according to Michael Nathans, president of Trycera Financial Credit Services. "A large segment of the population doesn't receive the most favorable rates or offers because they either don't have credit scores or their credit scores are too low. Having even one or two ECOA-qualified credit accounts added to your traditional credit reports and scores could change you from a denial to an approval, and save you thousands of dollars on an auto loan, for example."

So the next time you walk into a bank, bring your cable bills and cancelled checks in a shoebox. Hand them to the loan officer and tell them you're choosing to leverage your rights under ECOA Reg B and you want them to consider your cable payment history. They'll look at you like you're crazy, but if they give the box back without considering the paperwork, they'll be violating federal law.

CHAPTER 24

The CARD Act: The Good, Bad & Ugly

On May 22, 2009, President Obama signed the Credit Card Accountability, Responsibility, and Disclosure Act of 2009. This new law, better known as the Credit CARD Act, was implemented throughout 2009 and 2010. The purpose of the Act, as is common of many laws, is to protect consumers from deceptive practices and actions of the credit card industry. And while the Act was initially applauded as an improvement to consumer protections, the news isn't all good. In fact, when you slice the Act up provision by provision you can start to see where much of it is meaningless and even damaging in some instances.

A CARD ACT RECAP

The purpose of this section is to provide an overview of the CARD Act's protections and what they mean to you, the American credit card user.

Twenty-One-Day Grace Period

Your credit card issuer must now send you your statement a full twenty-one days before the due date. Before the CARD Act, grace periods had shrunk down to fourteen days. This additional week will help consumers who depend on their biweekly paycheck in order to pay their bills on time.

Under Twenty-One Years Old, No New Credit Cards

The CARD Act prevents credit card issuers from opening new accounts for consumers who are under twenty-one. There are two ways around the under-twenty-one rule. If you have a job or can prove you have the capacity to make your payments, then you can open a card. Or if you are able to convince someone to cosign for you, then you can open a card as well.

No More Over-Limit Fees

When you make a purchase that takes you over your credit limit, credit card issuers used to be able to charge you an over-limit fee, usually around $35. This is no longer allowed unless you give your credit card issuer permission to charge you the fee. If you do not, then any transaction that would take you over your credit limit will be denied at the register or point of sale.

Advance Notice for Adverse Changes to Your Credit Card Terms

If your credit card issuer wants to increase your interest rate, add a new fee, or increase an existing fee, they are still allowed to do so under most circumstances. However, they must notify you forty-five days in advance of making the change and allow you to "opt out." There are some exceptions to the forty-five-day rule. They are:

- If you have a variable interest rate, a rate tied to a moving index, and the index increases, then the card issuer does not have to notify you of the new higher rate.

- If you have an introductory or "teaser" rate that has expired, then the issuer does not have to notify you of the new higher rate.
- Additionally, if you choose to opt out of the new rate or new fee, then the issuer can close your card and accelerate the payback of the outstanding balance, and there is no acknowledgment provision regarding the forty-five-day notice. If they send it and you ignore it, trash it, or don't understand it, they've still complied with the law.

No Retroactive Rate Increases
Credit card issuers used to be able increase the interest rate on existing balances. This is not allowed any longer. If your credit card issuer increases your interest rate, then the new higher rate will only be applied to new purchases.

Late Fee Restrictions
Your late fee must be more in line with the amount of your delinquency. For example, if your minimum payment was only $12 and you were late, then the late fee cannot exceed $12. Late fees cannot exceed $35.

Pay Off and Interest Disclosure
Your credit card statement must now contain a chart or table clearly showing you how long it would take to pay off your credit card balance if you only make the minimum payment. And, it must also show you how much interest you'll pay by doing so. This has been hailed as the most valuable component of the CARD Act.

Inactivity Fees
You can no longer be charged a fee for card dormancy. These fees became moderately popular at the beginning of the credit crisis in late 2007. The credit card issuer can, however, close the account because of dormancy.

Interest Rate Decreases for On-Time Payments

If your credit card issuer increases your interest rate because of delinquency, then they must consider lowering your rate if you make payments on time for six consecutive months.

Gift Card Protections

Any gift card that was purchased after August 22, 2010, must follow these guidelines regarding expiration or reduction in value: The card must be good for a full five years from the date of purchase. Any fees charged to your card must be clearly disclosed to the purchaser. A dormancy fee can still be charged against the card's value, but only if you don't use the card for twelve consecutive months.

Free Credit Report Rule

This one was an interesting addition to the CARD Act, considering it has nothing to do with credit cards. Any website that markets a free credit report must now disclose that the free credit report they're giving away is not the same free credit report that is mandated under federal law and available via www.AnnualCreditReport.com.

Restriction on Some Overdraft Fees

This isn't a CARD Act provision, but it's applicable to debit and ATM cards, so I figured I'd throw it in. As of August 22, 2010, every single person in this country who had overdraft protection for debit cards and ATM cards usage lost it. And at the same time, the banks lost the ability to charge overdraft fees for debit card and ATM card usage that took you under the $0 mark on your account. You have to proactively opt back in if you want to continue to have the coverage. If you opt in, then the bank or credit union can once again charge you the overdraft fee. If you do not opt back in, then any transaction that would take you below $0 will be declined.

WHAT'S STILL ALLOWED UNDER THE CARD ACT

Now that we know what's no longer allowed under the CARD Act, let's take a look at what's still allowed . . .

Universal Default

This is the practice of increasing an interest rate because you missed a payment on another card. For example, the interest rate on Credit Card A goes up because you missed a payment on Credit Card B. This is still allowed under the CARD Act as long as the issuer of Credit Card A sends you a forty-five-day advance notice of the rate increase.

Credit Limit Reductions

Not only are credit limit reductions still fully allowed under the CARD Act, but no advance notice is required. The only notice that's required is pursuant to the Fair Credit Reporting Act's rules of Adverse Action. If a credit report or credit score is used as a basis for the reduction, then the issuer must send you a notice stating such. But the notice does not have to be sent in advance of the reduction.

Account Closures

Again, closures are fully allowed and no advance notice is required. However, the same adverse action rules explained above apply with account closures. The credit card industry argued that giving consumers forty-five-day advance notice of credit limit reductions or account closures would lead to card-holders maxing out their cards to avoid losing the benefit of the "open to buy."

SUCCESSES, FAILURES, AND MYTHS
OF THE CARD ACT

On February 22, 2011, the bulk of the Credit Card Account-ability, Responsibility, and Disclosure Act (CARD Act) turned a year old. It's time to take inventory of some of its successes and failures, and, like you know I love to do, bust a myth at the same time.

Success: Identity Theft Is Down, in Part Because of the Act

Identity theft incidents were down 28 percent in 2010 from 2009, according to Javelin Strategy and Research. And the newly released "Top Consumer Complaints in 2010" statistics from the Federal Trade Commission show that the number of complaints about identity theft dropped from 278,078 in 2009 to 250,854 in 2010. It's still the number one complaint, but not by as much as in the past. Debt collector complaints are catching up (shocking).

It was an unintended side effect, but the CARD Act can take some credit for the reduction in identity theft incidents and complaints. The Act made it illegal for credit card issuers to charge over-limit fees on credit card transactions that took your balance over your predetermined credit limit. So, in reaction, the credit card industry simply declines those transactions because of their inability to hit you with the $35 over-limit fee.

What that meant was any thief who swiped your card and then tried to buy something expensive enough to take you over the limit was unsuccessful because the transaction was denied at the register. In the past those same fraudulent transactions could have been approved because the card issuer could charge the fee. Thanks, CARD Act!

Failure: Advance Notice Is Not Required for Account Closures or Credit Limit Decreases

Every once in a while I have a hard time writing about something because it seems so unbelievable. This is one of those times. The CARD Act requires forty-five-day advance notice for adverse changes to the terms of your credit cardholder's agreement. Sounds great, right?

The problem is that two of what I would define as *the* most adverse changes do *not* require any advance notice, at all. The first is credit limit reductions. The issuer is not required to give you any advance notice if they lower your credit limit. They *do* have to send you something if the reduction was done because of your credit reports or scores. But that can come *after* the limit has already been reduced.

The second is account closure. There is no requirement to notify you in advance that "Hey, we're going to close your account in forty-five days . . . *heads up!*" There is, again, an obligation to eventually notify you, but only if your credit was the basis for their decision.

This was a win for the credit card industry because they feared that if you told someone about an upcoming closure or line reduction, then they would charge up their card in advance. I'm not sure I agree with them. I don't know many people who would max their cards out of spite.

Failure: CARD Act Has a Disproportionate Negative Impact on Women

The CARD Act was billed as protecting consumers from their credit card issuers. However, in an ironic twist of poorly thought-out legislation, the CARD Act can have a disproportionate negative impact on stay-at-home wives, by preventing them from opening credit cards on their own without a husband's cosignature. It also affects stay-at-home husbands, but on a smaller scale.

One of the provisions of the CARD Act is the requirement that a credit card issuer verify income or "capacity" (the ability to pay) before allowing someone to open a new account. If no income is present, a cosigner is required. The wording is meant to eliminate students who are under twenty-one from opening a new credit card and getting into credit card debt. The hypothesis makes sense: let's make sure people who don't have an income won't get into a bunch of credit card debt they can't afford. The problem is the enormous number of people who choose not to work, and thus have no income, yet engage in commerce on behalf of their family or household.

The issue is the Act's requirement that creditors consider only the individual applicant's income, rather than the applicant's household income. Zero individual income means zero credit card approval, despite the possibility that the applicant does, in fact, have access to funds through a working spouse. What's even worse is the requirement that a cosigner also apply for the card, which results in dual liability for payment and dual risk for any negative credit reporting because of nonpayment.

This certainly isn't the first time women have been unfairly, and unintentionally, on the wrong end of a credit-related law or policy. Remember when FICO was going to eliminate the evaluation of "authorized user" credit card accounts in their newest FICO score, FICO 08? They were reacting to the large number, at that time, of credit repair companies that were selling access to credit card accounts in an attempt to game their scoring system. In that instance, many women, who are authorized users on their husband's credit cards more often than vice versa, would have seen their scores go down or disappear altogether. Thankfully, FICO figured out another way to protect their scores from gaming, and the potential issue was eliminated.

In addition to women and men who don't work, this is going to hurt commerce and retailers. Anyone who applies for store credit to finance a major retail purchase better have a job. And anyone who wants a credit limit increase in order to fund a larger purchase, which might be completely affordable to them, better have a job.

This is why many retailers, not just those who sell products targeted to women, are balking at the "individual income" provision. And they're right. Think about all of the parents who tell their kids to go out and open a new gas card in their name so they can learn how to manage their own credit cards. This learning experience is all but eliminated by not only the "income" requirement of the CARD Act, but also the "under twenty-one" restrictions under the same law.

I don't know about you, but this angers me and I'm not a stay-at-home dad, and neither is my wife a stay-at-home mom. I imagine this is going to anger anyone who chooses not to work, for whatever reason. And lastly, this really should bother anyone who believes a woman (or a man) shouldn't have to formally depend on their spouse for "financial confirmation."

And if you really think this is actually a good idea because it's a sufficient hurdle to getting into credit card debt, think again. There's the issue of someone simply choosing to use an existing credit card account, because existing accounts are not affected by this CARD Act income rule. The Act also assumes that people are going to simply give up after they've been told they need an income to qualify. Name one "avoidance" law in the history of history that has ever succeeded. Prohibition, drinking age, driving age, controlled substances, immigration . . . have any of them really worked?

People are still going to open and use credit cards, and can you guess why? They're going to open and use cards because they want to. And if history has taught us anything, it's that people who want to do something bad enough are going to figure out a way to do so, regardless of the legality.

This "no income" silliness is going to lead to dishonesty, fraud, and "just add my spouse's name" cosigning. How many of you cosigners out there remember signing anything for your credit card accounts? If you look at the online applications, they don't require a second "acknowledgment." They simply allow you to add a name to the account. You can stop laughing now.

The question isn't "how should the law be changed to allow for household income?" The question should be "how can we eliminate the entire 'under twenty-one' and 'income proof' requirements of the CARD Act in their entirety?" It's one of the most nonsensical provisions and assumes that avoidance is the same as protection.

These types of protections are very poorly thought out by people who, frankly, don't know squat about the mechanics of consumer credit. They sound good in a chamber ("Hey, let's require income in order to get a credit card!"), but the devil is always in the details. I strongly believe the CARD Act will eventually go down in history as one of the worst consumer protection laws ever written because of the aforementioned (and several other) unintended difficulties. If I've said it once, I've said it a thousand times: when it comes to the government protecting me, please ... protect me from Al-Qaeda, I'll protect myself from credit card issuers.

Failure: The Government Tries to Protect Young'ins from Evil Credit Card Issuers with the Under Twenty-One Rule

Everyone has an opinion about credit cards. They're great and they're terrible and they're everything in between, depending on whom you ask. But one thing is certain: we adults have always had the right to apply for, open, and use credit cards as we saw fit, so long as we were old enough to sign a contract, which we can do when we're eighteen. Now we no longer enjoy the privilege to make up our own minds on this matter.

Thanks to the CARD Act, you can no longer open a credit card account until you're twenty-one years old, unless you have a job or a cosigner. This is the law of the land since February 22, 2011. The question is, was this the right move? How old should you have to be before you walk around with your very own credit card, no strings attached? What exactly was accomplished?

I've always found these age-based "forced avoidance" rules somewhat humorous and extremely nonsensical, especially when there is no scientific basis for the age cutoff. It's a statistical fact that drivers are better insurance risks when they're over twenty-five, so that makes sense because it saves rental car companies money. Stipulated! But where is the evidence that supports that a twenty-one-year-old is a better manager of credit cards than an eighteen-, nineteen-, or twenty-year-old? You can stop looking, because it doesn't exist.

What *does* exist is a mountain of evidence showing that this provision of the CARD Act not only doesn't make any sense, but is in fact problematic. Follow me . . .

"Avoidance" Doesn't Equal "Education"   I promise that no credit epiphany occurs at age twenty-one. I know plenty of credit-savvy twenty-one-year-olds and even more credit disasters pushing fifty. Proper credit management knows no age boundary, yet someone felt it necessary to make you wait the three additional years to either be responsible or not. There is also no new requirement to take a "Credit Cards 101" class in either high school or college, yet it's hard to argue that it's not more important than history, music, art, psychology, or physical education.

Cosigning = BAD IDEA   The CARD Act actually allows a lender to issue you a credit card as long as your parent cosigns for you, regardless of your age or income. What this means is both of you would now be equally liable for the debt and equally at risk for credit damage if the card is mismanaged in any way. For example, if your parent runs up a balance on the card, your credit will suffer. If you think your parent is making the payments on time, and they aren't, your credit will suffer. If these things happen, you won't be able to simply change your mind about being on the account, because the lender won't let one of you jump off the liability train. Lending 101 = two liable parties is better than one liable party.

Additionally, if your parent has poor credit, then you could very well be declined outright or saddled with adverse terms. So, the penalty for being under twenty-one could be a 29 percent interest rate on your revolving balances, thanks to Mom or Dad. And you can't earn a better rate by properly managing the account, because the lender is under no obligation to adjust it downward, ever.

No, I think it's safe to say that this part of the CARD Act was the legislative equivalent of a "swing and a miss." I get the hypothesis: you restrict credit card usage by young people and you prevent them from getting into debt. Nobody likes to see people in debt, let alone young people. But this isn't going to prevent that from happening. It just delays it from happening for three years.

Myth: Universal Default Has Been Eliminated

Universal default, the process whereby a credit card issuer jacks up your interest rate because of something you did with a completely different card, was handicapped by the Act, but not eliminated, as many believe. The only component of old-fashioned universal default that was eliminated was the retroactive interest rate increase, where they'd increase rates on existing balances. Thankfully, that has been eliminated.

Other components of universal default still live on. If the card is over a year old, then issuers can still increase your rates for any reason, as long as they give you the forty-five-day notice. Even still, if your card has an expiring teaser rate or is tied to a moving index (the so-called "variable rate" card), then no notice is required before the increase.

So, if you miss a payment on your John's Bank Credit Card, your Dave's Bank Card can increase your rate. And if your FICO score drops, for whatever reason, they can all increase your rates as well.

CARD ACT INCOME RULES: ALTERNATIVE OPTIONS FOR STAY-AT-HOME MOMS AND DADS AND PEOPLE UNDER TWENTY-ONE

If you are in the position of not having an income and you want to be able to get some plastic, here are the ethical workarounds.

Become an Authorized User

As I covered earlier, an authorized user is someone who has a card with his or her name on it, but who doesn't have financial liability for the payments (except in certain instances in community property states). They do, however, have full charging privileges, just like the primary cardholder. The card does show up on their credit reports, in many cases, so being an authorized user is a great way to establish credit or rebuild credit.

Think of it like having a credit card with training wheels. It's a great way for young people to begin their credit journey. Or it's a way around the CARD Act provision that prevents issuers from opening a card for someone who has no income. The "authorized user" strategy is a generally accepted method of getting some plastic in your wallet . . . just be responsible with it!

Find a Cosigner

This is a dangerous road, so I caution anyone who chooses this option. In fact, we're now seeing students cosigning for other students in order to get credit cards. Wow, that's bad news, and it supports my comment from earlier that people are going to find a way to get a card if they want one badly enough.

In many cases, the cosigner is going to be a spouse, which might seem completely benign. However, with 50 percent of marriages ending in divorce, it's a chance that about half of you will wish you hadn't taken. Again, as discussed in Chapter 5, co-mingling debts is easy . . . de-mingling them is next to impossible. And in a divorce scenario, "working together" to separate debts (a requirement of the card issuer) seems unrealistic.

Find a Job

Yes, I know this makes all the sense in the world. No income should equal no credit card, right? Trust me, it's just not that simple. Hit a popular area mall at 2 p.m. on a Tuesday during the school year and an overwhelming percentage of the people you'll see are stay-at-home moms and dads, who have no individual income. Eliminating their ability to get credit on behalf of their household seems unfair to me.

Certainly you can get a job and then "work" your way around the income requirement provision (pardon the pun). I just don't think it's realistic to expect someone to go to a retail outlet, be denied a card because of no income, go find a job, and then come back to reapply. It's so much easier to . . .

. . . Use Another Card

The income requirement, thankfully, only applies to new accounts. It doesn't apply to the continued use of an existing credit card account. The CARD Act police are not going to knock on your door and take away your cards if you can't produce a pay stub. To me this is the very reason why the income requirement makes no sense. Instead of allowing the "buyer" to open a new account and save 15–20 percent off the purchase, we're going to force them to use an existing card, at no discount. They'll spend *more*, not less.

I realize there are good reasons to keep certain people away from plastic. In fact, there are some people who shouldn't have credit of any kind . . . ever. But to simply make it a rule that an income is required in order to open a card, which doesn't mean you'll ever use it or ever revolve a balance, seems like a nuclear approach to a surgical problem. I'll always err on the side that thinks educating someone, be they under twenty-one or a stay-at-home spouse, on the dangers of plastic use is a teaching opportunity that pays immeasurable dividends.

CHAPTER 25

Fair Debt Collection Practices

The Fair Debt Collection Practices Act (FDCPA) was enacted in 1977. It's the federal law that protects consumers from abusive collection practices by third-party debt collectors. There are also many states that have similar protective statutes. For example, those of you who live in California enjoy the FDCPA protections as well as those afforded to you by the Rosenthal Act. I certainly hope you'll never have to deal with collection agencies, but if you do, it's important that you understand these rights under the federal act.

COMMUNICATION MUST OCCUR AT CONVENIENT HOURS

Collectors may not contact debtors before 8 a.m. or after 9 p.m. local time, based on where the consumer is located. That means no calls at 8 a.m. Eastern Time to a debtor living in Texas and no calls at 10 p.m. Eastern Time from a collector working in California.

CALLS CANNOT BE MADE TO THE DEBTOR'S WORKPLACE

There is an exception to this rule. If you give the collector permission to contact you at work or if communicating with you at work isn't disallowed by your employer then, in general, it's allowed. If you tell the collector that you are not allowed to receive calls at work, or if you could get in trouble because of their calls, then they must stop.

DISCLOSURE TO THIRD PARTIES IS NOT ALLOWED

In general, the collector is not allowed to communicate with anyone other than the debtor regarding the debt. In other words, the collector can't call your neighbors and tell them that you owe $5,000 in past-due credit card charges. I've had some interesting cases where I've served as an expert witness that have included evidence of messages left on answering machines. It was argued that this is a violation of this provision because someone other than the debtor was able to listen to the messages.

THEY MUST STOP IF YOU ASK THEM

Despite beliefs to the contrary, consumers can actually demand that the collector stop communicating with them. This must be done in writing, not verbally. So, you can't just tell them "I demand that you stop calling me." There are two exceptions to this rule. The collector may contact the debtor after they've received a valid written demand to cease communications to let the debtor know that the collector is not attempting to collect the debt any longer. And they may also notify the debtor that they'll attempt other methods normally used by collectors to collect debt. Read between the lines: this means a potential lawsuit from a collection attorney.

NO ABUSIVE BEHAVIOR

We've all seen the hidden videos where collectors are threatening to have you thrown in jail or to take away your children if you don't pay your debts. This is clearly not allowed. They are also not allowed to threaten violence, use profanity or insensitive remarks, publish your name as someone who won't pay their bills (credit reporting is an exception), or call you over and over in an abusive manner. I had a case where the collector called the consumer over 200 times in one year. Is that abusive? Before you answer, remember that 200 calls over 365 days is much less than one phone call per day. What do you think?

THEY MUST DISCLOSE WHO THEY ARE

If you've ever received a call from a debt collector, it was probably prefaced with "I'm calling from XYZ and the purpose of this call is to collect a debt." And if you've ever received a letter from a collection agency, it probably had language that disclosed that the communication was from a debt collector and that any information they receive could be used in furtherance of collecting a debt. These are required disclosures. They can't sneak up on you.

NO MISREPRESENTATIONS

What gets a collector in hot water very quickly is any act of dishonesty. Collectors are not allowed to:

- Imply that they are with a governmental organization
- Misrepresent the balance of the debt
- Pretend to be an attorney
- Imply that nonpayment will result in garnishment unless the collector intends to pursue garnishment
- Threaten legal action if none is intended
- Imply that not paying debt is a criminal offense

MUST SHOW THE DEBT AS IN DISPUTE, IF IT IS

This is an obligation under the Fair Credit Reporting Act (FCRA). If the debtor challenges the validity of the collection, the collection agency must show the account as being in dispute not only within their own records, but also along with the account as reported to your credit files. This is a fairly common FCRA violation in the cases I've been involved with.

There are actually several more rules outlined in the FDCPA, but these are the highlights and the more common violations. In fact, according to WebRecon, there were 10,858 FDCPA lawsuits in 2010, which is 1,715 more than in 2009. The pace in 2011 suggests that there will be 12,000 filed. So, what do you think? Any interest in owning a collection agency?

CHAPTER 26

Fair Access to Credit Scores Act

On July 21, 2011, consumers gained access to their actual credit scores under several very common scenarios. Here's the back story:

In March 2010, senator Mark Udall (D-CO) introduced the Fair Access to Credit Scores Act of 2010. The Act was swept up in the legislation referred to as the Dodd-Frank Wall Street Reform and Consumer Protection Act, which means it became effective July 21, 2011. And on July 6, 2011, the Federal Reserve Board and the Federal Trade Commission issued final rules regarding the credit score disclosure regulations, which clarified the conditions under which consumers would have access to their credit score. Here's an overview:

CREDIT SCORE DISCLOSURE IS REQUIRED *BY LENDERS* IF:

- A consumer applies for credit, gets approved, and a credit score is used to set the material terms of the account. This applies if your lender chooses what's referred to as the "Credit Score Disclosure" notice as a way to comply with the new rules.

- A consumer applies for credit and is denied credit based on a credit score. You'll get a declination letter and your score, as well as information about where you can claim your free credit report used by the lender to make their decision.

- A consumer applies for credit and gets approved but with less advantageous terms compared to the terms other approved applicants were given. This is a practice commonly referred to as risk-based pricing (see Chapter 13).

- A consumer has an existing account with a credit card issuer and the annual percentage rate is increased based on a credit score.

- A consumer applies for a mortgage loan. This has actually been a requirement since the 2003 amendment to the Fair Credit Reporting Act, but I wanted to throw it in here just to remind you.

IMPORTANT: Every one of the scenarios above is automatic. You do not have to ask your lenders for your scores. They must send them to you proactively. This is significantly different from the free credit report rules, which require *you* to ask for your federally mandated free credit reports. This means you should keep your eyes open for letters from your lenders because they may have your credit scores included.

CREDIT SCORE DISCLOSURE IS *NOT* REQUIRED IF:

- A consumer applies for insurance, utilities, or rental housing and the score used is not the same style of score used by lenders to make loan-specific decisions. This does not constitute a "credit score" as defined by the Fair Credit Reporting Act, because the law defines a credit score as a score used for the purposes of lending money, and only credit scores are required to be disclosed.

- A lender bases a lending decision solely on a "proprietary score," which is a score that is developed by a creditor for their use only (versus those built by FICO, for example). The exception is if the proprietary scoring model uses only information from a credit bureau to generate the score. If so, then it must be disclosed.
- A lender uses multiple scores that meet the definition of a "credit score." In that case, the lender has the option to choose to disclose only one of the scores rather than all of the scores.

In addition to the scores, the consumer will likely be given information about the score range from which credit bureau the score came, where they rank nationally compared to other consumers, and how to obtain a copy of their credit report for free.

The score disclosure may not clearly identify the "brand" or type of score the lender used to make their decision, so the consumer will have to rely on the disclosed score range to determine what score was used. If the range is 300 to 850, then a FICO score was used. If the range is 501 to 990, then a VantageScore was used.

WHO GETS LEFT OUT IN THE COLD

Neither the risk-based pricing rules nor the FACS Act allow for us to get free copies of our credit scores annually like we can get our free credit reports annually through www.AnnualCreditReport.com. You have to at least apply for something in order for the free score to be a possibility. The argument is that if you've been approved for whatever you're applying for at the best rate, then you have good enough scores and have less of a reason to see them.

Eh, I'm not sure I agree with that argument.

CHAPTER 27

Medical Debt Responsibility
Act of 2011

On June 2, 2011, representatives Don Manzullo (R-IL), Ralph Hall (R-TX), and Heath Shuler (D-NC) introduced the Medical Debt Responsibility Act of 2011. The Act would require the removal of medical collections from credit reports if they are paid in full, settled in full, and are less than $2,500. The removal would have to take place within forty-five days of payment.

The introduction of this legislation has its pros and cons, and politicians and industry stalwarts seem to disagree on the value of medical debt to lenders and risk managers. According to representative Nydia Velazquez (D-NY), "Medical debt is not a reliable indicator of credit risk, yet nearly a quarter of Americans have seen their credit scores plummet because of small, routine medical bills." However, Lisa Nelson from FICO writes on their *Banking Analytics Blog*, "FICO research repeatedly shows that records of such credit activities [medical collection records] are highly predictive of credit risk for years after the fact." Who do you believe, the politician or the statistician?

The proposed legislation will have huge bipartisan political and nonpolitical support, which is no surprise. The prospect of getting negative information removed from credit reports will be popular with consumers, consumer groups, and any entity that depends on the brokering of loans to make a living. The potential problem with this tinkering of credit report data is the long-term downside.

If you disallow lenders to consider highly predictive information, such as medical collections, then they're simply going to subsidize their risk by charging higher rates and fees to everyone. And if you don't believe this can happen, all you have to do is look at the lending industry's reaction to the CARD Act and other legislation that chokes their ability to make money. Interest rates on credit cards are now at a ten-year high, nearly 15 percent.

Insurance regulations already require scoring systems to bypass any medically related item on a credit report. There's also momentum at the state level to disallow credit reports to be used by employers for the screening of applicants. Federal tax liens that are paid in full and withdrawn must be taken off credit reports, new since the new IRS rules regarding tax lien withdrawals.

Credit reports are certainly not the most popular items in our lives, unless you've got great credit. But they do serve an invaluable purpose for companies that choose to go "at risk" by letting you borrow money, live in their apartments, have their insurance, or work for their companies. Eliminating predictive and accurate credit report information simply because some people don't want it there is a dangerous step in the wrong direction back toward a time when credit decisions took weeks to make and were subject to nonscientific underwriting procedures.

PART VII

Planning Ahead & the Future of Credit

CHAPTER 28

Your Next Application & the Future of Consumer Credit

Before we wrap up and conclude this book, I wanted to give you something practical, something that can save you a boat-load of money in the future. Before you fill out your next job, credit, or insurance application, I want you to remember the following five credit questions and be sure to ask the appropriate questions from this list.

YOUR NEXT CREDIT CARD APPLICATION

Question 1: "Do You Report Credit Limits to the Credit Bureaus?"

Missing credit limits can lead to lower credit scores and some credit card issuers do not report your credit limits. The problem used to be much worse years ago when Capital One with-held credit limits on their accounts. They started reporting limits in 2007 and have largely been forgiven for withholding the important data. There are, however, still some cards where limits won't be reported. The so-called "no limit" cards don't report limits and charge cards don't report limits.

This is important because the credit limit (as reported on your credit file) is the denominator in the "revolving debt utilization" calculation. And if it's missing, then the "highest balance ever" figure is used in lieu of the limit. If the highest balance ever figure isn't as high as the credit limit, and it generally isn't unless you've maxed out your card, then your utilization percentage will be higher, and your credit score could be lower. So, asking the question up front could save your scores. Here's a really damaging example:

Credit Limit: $10,000

High Balance: $1,000

Current Balance: $900

In that example, the **real** utilization is 9 percent ($900/$10,000), not bad at all. But if that limit were missing, then the utilization would be 90 percent ($900/$1,000), which is terrible. This measurement is taken on a line item (card by card) basis *and* an aggregate (all cards) basis, so there's no escaping the damage.

YOUR NEXT EMPLOYMENT APPLICATION

Question 2: "Do You Review Credit Reports When You Screen Potential Employees?"

Employers are allowed, in most states, to review your credit reports as part of employment screening. They're required by law to get your permission to do so. It still is a good idea to ask up front if they intend to do so.

If you're like millions of other Americans, then your credit is in the tank. Thirty-five percent of the population has FICO scores under 650 and while scores are **not** used by employers—reports yes, scores no—the data underlying a 650 (and below) isn't flattering, which means that 35 percent of the population has poor credit. The worst thing that could happen would be to not get a job, or waste time and energy pursuing one, if your credit is going to disqualify you for consideration.

Knowing in advance will give you the opportunity to work on your explanation. And if your report contains damaging errors, it will give you time to get them corrected. If the company is hiring for multiple positions, it might even allow you to choose a role that is "credit free."

YOUR NEXT LOAN (OR INSURANCE) APPLICATION

Question 3: "Which Credit Bureau Do You Use?"

Why would you want to know this before you applied for a loan or insurance? The answer is very simple: strategic applying. If you knew that your FICO score from Equifax was 700 and your FICO score from TransUnion was 645, and you knew the lender used TransUnion for their credit reports, wouldn't you want to maybe find a lender who used Equifax?

You would be more likely to get approved and more likely to get approved with better terms. Many consumers assume that lenders won't tell them what credit bureau they use. Some don't, but some do. It's not a national security breach for Joe's Bank to tell you that they use Equifax for their credit reports. They might even tell you what minimum score they require to approve the type of loan you're interested in. Arming yourself with this information can save you the embarrassment of a denial *and* the potential damage of the wasted credit inquiry.

Question 4: "Which Score Are You Using?"

This is different than knowing **what** score your lender requires for an approval. This is finding out which **version** of score they're using. There are many different versions of the FICO scoring software and not all lenders are using the most current version, to your detriment.

The newest version of the FICO score is still called, unofficially, FICO 08. This version does **not** count collections that have an original balance of less than $100. This version also scores low-risk consumers higher than older versions. Point being, if you're a good borrower, you *really* want your lender to use the FICO 08 version.

You can't force your lender to use this version, and the entire mortgage industry is still years behind when it comes to adopting newer scoring models. Fannie Mae and Freddie Mac—that's about 70 percent of all mortgages—are still using older, much older, versions that were built well before the credit crisis. There are lenders who are using current scoring versions and you should take your business to them.

Question 5: "What Is the Minimum Score Required to Get Approved at the Best Rate?"

Guess what happened in July 2011? The FACS Act (Fair Access to Credit Scores Act) went into effect. And boy oh boy, was I counting the days! This law requires lenders to give you, for free, the actual score they used if they declined you. This will lead to a new era of score transparency.

We should soon have enough data to put together tables for every lender that answers the question, "What minimum score do I need to get approved?" If XYZ Bank declines you at 647, it won't be a secret any longer. Point being, we'll be able to cobble together a really good understanding of minimum score requirements thanks to the FACS Act.

So don't be shy the next time you're about to fill out that application. Asking one or two questions can save you money on a loan, save you some embarrassment, and make you sound like a well-informed consumer.

FINAL THOUGHTS

That's it. You're done with my second book. I hope you found it to be educational and worth your time and money. And rather than just leaving you with "the end," I wanted to give you some closing thoughts:

1. Credit is often maligned and criticized, sometimes for good reasons and sometimes for poor reasons. But despite what you may hear from credit "celebrities," we *need* credit to function efficiently. So, my suggestion is for you to focus your energy on learning how the system works so you can benefit from it. Taking the time to read this book was a step in the right direction.

2. Credit scoring isn't going away any time soon. This is where I'm supposed to tell you to "get used to it, 'cause it ain't gonna change." Rather than tell you that, I'll simply say that there is no better method of assessing your credit risk than a credit score. It offers a balance between efficient, cost-effective underwriting and consumer demand for fast and affordable credit access.

3. Proper credit management is an effective way to build wealth. As I pointed out in my first book, *You're Nothing But a Number,* paying more for things you're going to finance is really no different than picking a bad stock or investing in the wrong "opportunity." We all have our bottom lines, and whatever helps to grow that bottom line, legally, should be considered an important facet of our wealth-building activities. Paying $1,000 for a mortgage instead of $1,250 for the same house is just as effective as picking an investment that grows at a guaranteed rate of $3,000 per year. Do the math.

Index